Bugs in
ORIGAMI

Bugs in ORIGAMI

John Montroll

Dover Publications, Inc.
New York

To Paul and Constantin

Bibliographical Note

Bugs in Origami is a new work, first published
by Dover Publications, Inc., in 2013.

Library of Congress Cataloging-in-Publication Data

Montroll, John.
 Bugs in origami / John Montroll.
    pages cm
 ISBN-13: 978-0-486-49884-3 (alk. paper)
 ISBN-10: 0-486-49884-0 (alk. paper)
 1. Origami. 2. Insects in art. I. Title.
 TT872.5.M648   2013
 736'.982–dc23   2013026714

Manufactured in the United States by Courier Corporation
49884001   2013
www.doverpublications.com

Introduction

ugs are fascinating creatures and challenging subjects to fold. Here is a collection of over twenty favorite bugs including a fly, dragonfly, praying mantis, grasshopper, hornet, centipede, spider, several beetles and more. Each model is folded from a single square sheet of paper with no cutting. Most insects have six legs, wings, and antennae, making these models complex or very complex to fold. Such models should be folded from large paper at least 10 inches square.

Designing complex insects has been a recent development in origami. My early origami books in the 1980's were among the first such books to show how to fold complex bugs with full appendages from a single uncut square. This new level of complexity influenced the origami world and started a movement of technical folding and of designing very complex insects. Throughout the world, origami designers developed models requiring well over one to two hundred steps to fold. Many of those designs use a technique of box-pleating where the first steps divide the square paper in a grid of vertical and horizontal creases, such as 48 x 48.

I have taken great care to present a collection of complex bugs, yet kept them easy enough to be folded in less than one hundred steps. Some of the models, such as the praying mantis, have less than fifty steps. Box-pleating is not used. Several models, such as the hornet, use clever structures to allow detail, yet keep the number of steps to a minimum.

Each model is accompanied with a photograph and description. There is also an entertaining page on 'Appreciating Bugs'. As this full-color book is part of a series to simplify the organization of other books, some of the models were in older books.

The diagrams are drawn in the internationally approved Randlett-Yoshizawa style, which is easy to follow once you have learned the basic folds. You can use any kind of square paper for these models, but the best results can be achieved using standard origami paper, which is colored on one side and white on the other. In these diagrams, shading represents the colored side. Large sheets are easier to use than small ones. Origami supplies can be found in arts and craft shops, or at Dover Publications online: www.doverpublications.com. You can also visit OrigamiUSA at www.origamiusa.org for origami supplies and other related information including an extensive list of local, national, and international origami groups.

Many people helped to make this book possible. I thank Constantin Miranda for photographing several models. I thank Paul Aihe for some of the descriptions of the bugs. I thank my editors, Charley Montroll and Himanshu Agrawal. I also thank the many folders who proofread the diagrams.

John Montroll

www.johnmontroll.com

Contents

★   Simple
★★   Intermediate
★★★   Complex
★★★★ Very Complex

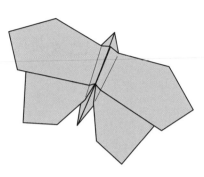

Simple Butterfly 14
★★

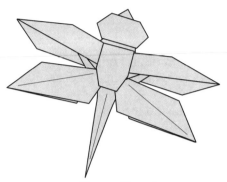

Dragonfly 16
★★

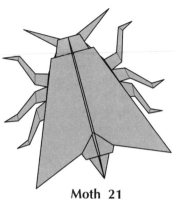

Moth 21
★★★

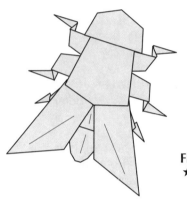

Fly 26
★★★

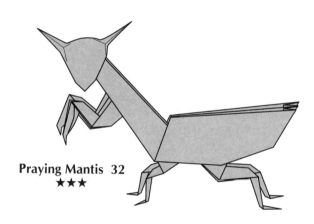

Praying Mantis 32
★★★

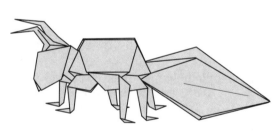

Hornet 38
★★★

Ant 43
★★★

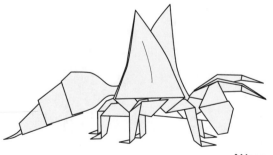

Wasp 44
★★★

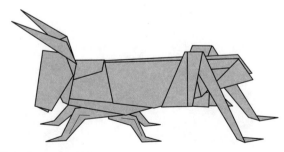

Grasshopper 51
★★★

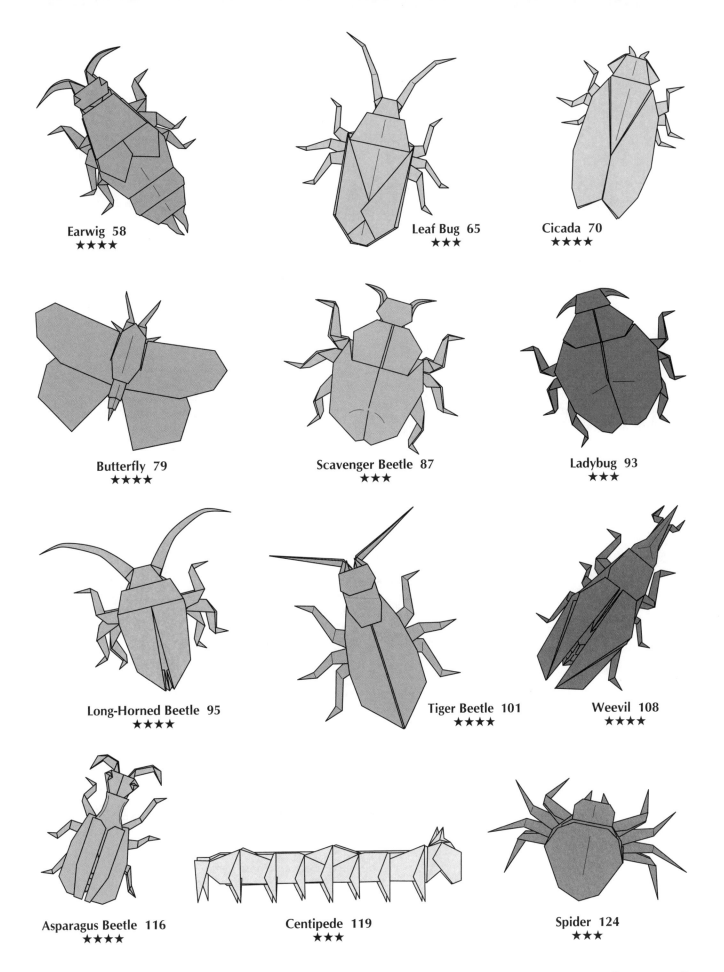

Symbols

Lines

— — — — — — — —   Valley fold, fold in front.

— · — · · — · — · · — · —   Mountain fold, fold behind.

————————————   Crease line.

···   X-ray or guide line.

Arrows

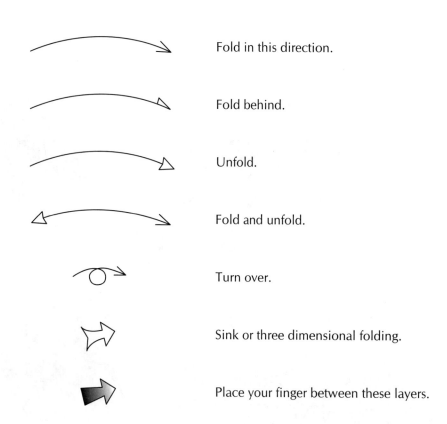

Fold in this direction.

Fold behind.

Unfold.

Fold and unfold.

Turn over.

Sink or three dimensional folding.

Place your finger between these layers.

Basic Folds

Pleat Fold.

Fold back and forth. Each pleat is composed of one valley and mountain fold. Here are two examples.

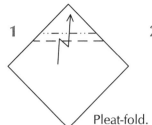 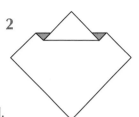

Pleat-fold.

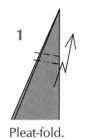 

Pleat-fold.

Squash Fold.

In a squash fold, some paper is opened and then made flat. The shaded arrow shows where to place your finger.

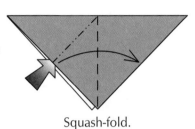 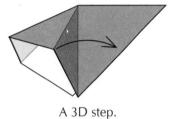 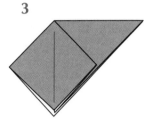

Squash-fold.   A 3D step.

Petal Fold.

In a petal fold, one point is folded up while two opposite sides meet each other.

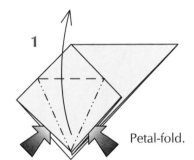 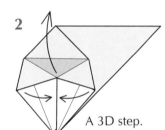 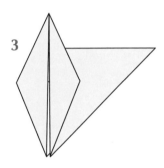

Petal-fold.   A 3D step.

Rabbit Ear.

To fold a rabbit ear, one corner is folded in half and laid down to a side.

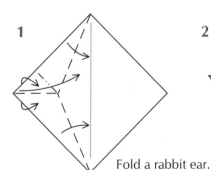 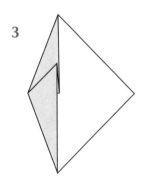

Fold a rabbit ear.   A 3D step.

Double Rabbit Ear.

If you were to bend a straw you would be folding the double rabbit ear.

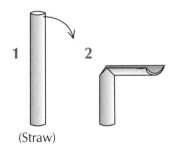 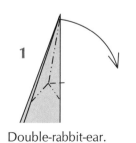 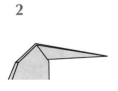

(Straw)   Double-rabbit-ear.

Inside Reverse Fold.

In an inside reverse fold, some paper is folded between layers. Here are two examples.

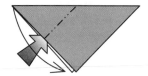

Reverse-fold.

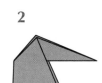

Reverse-fold.

Outside Reverse Fold.

Much of the paper must be unfolded to make an outside reverse fold.

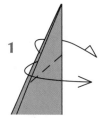

Outside-reverse-fold.

Crimp Fold.

A crimp fold is a combination of two reverse folds. Open the model slightly to form the crimp evenly on each side. Here are two examples.

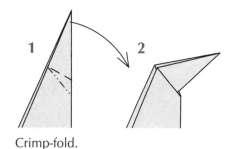

Crimp-fold.

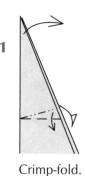
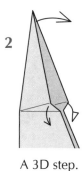

Crimp-fold.   A 3D step.

Sink.

For a sink, some of the paper without edges is folded inside. To do this fold, much of the model must be unfolded.

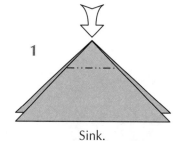

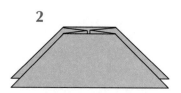

Sink.

Spread Squash Fold.

A cross between a squash fold and sink fold, some paper in the center is spread apart and then made flat.

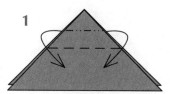

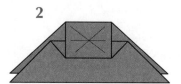

Spread-squash-fold.

Preliminary Fold.

The Preliminary Fold is the starting point for many models. The maneuver in step 3 occurs in many other models.

1
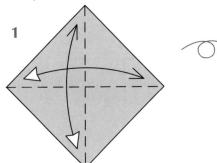
Fold and unfold.

2
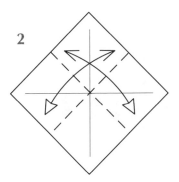
Fold and unfold.

3
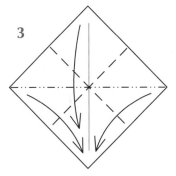
Collapse the square by bringing the four corners together.

4
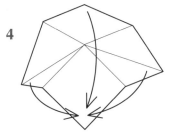
This is 3D.

5
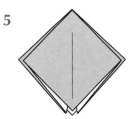
Preliminary Fold

Bird Base.

Historically, the Bird Base has been a very popular starting point. The folds used in it occur in many models.

1
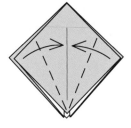
Begin with the Preliminary Fold. Kite-fold, repeat behind.

2
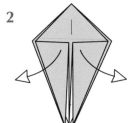
Unfold, repeat behind.

3
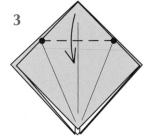

4
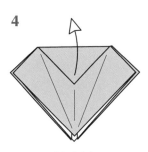
Unfold.

5
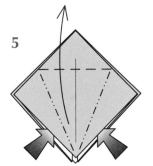
Petal-fold, repeat behind.

6
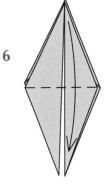
Repeat behind.

7
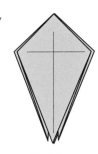
Bird Base

Blintz Frog Base.

This uses the double unwrap fold which is shown in detail below.

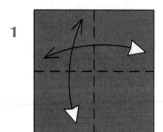

1

Fold and unfold.

2

Blintz fold: Fold the four corners to the center.

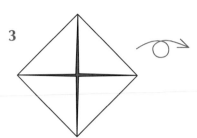

3

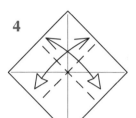

4

Fold and unfold.

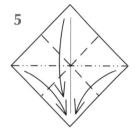

5

This is similar to the Preliminary Fold.

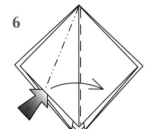

6

(Diagram enlarged.) Squash-fold.

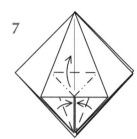

7

Petal-fold.

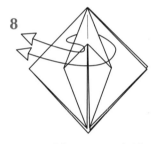

8

Double-unwrap-fold.

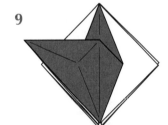

9

Repeat steps 6–8 three more times, on the back and sides.

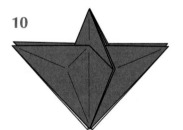

10

Blintz Frog Base

Double Unwrap Fold.

In the double unwrap fold, locked layers are unwrapped and refolded. Much of the folding is 3D. The diagrams are depicted as shown in steps 8 and 9 of the Blintz Frog Base.

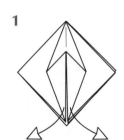

1

Begin with step 8 of the Blintz Frog Base. Spread at the bottom.

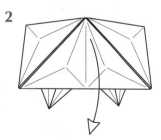

2

Unfold the top layer.

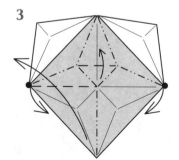

3

Refold along the creases. The dots will meet at the bottom.

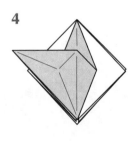

4

Appreciating Bugs

Bugs fill our world with beauty, wonder, and mystery. Insects, spiders, and other small multi-legged creatures are found in abundance on almost any land mass and by fresh-waters. There are over a million species of bugs, which is greater than the sum of all plants and other animal species. Our lives depend on the work of these small, productive, eco-friendly creatures.

Bugs are very colorful with a variety of interesting patterns and shapes. It is a joy to be surrounded by butterflies and ladybugs. Many insects use their color patterns and shapes as camouflage. As we enjoy their colors, they in turn can see a variety of colors beyond ours, including infrared and ultraviolet.

Plants and insects work together. Flowering plants depend on insects to pollinate them. These plants have varying colors and smells to attract specific insects. Even agricultural crops such as apples, blueberries, and melons depend on insect pollinators.

Insects eat decomposed material which recycles waste and fertilizes the ground. Spiders and bugs eat pests, such as harmful insects or weeds, which are destructive to vegetation. While bugs are important to plant-life, they are also food for birds, frogs, and other animals. Their small size is a definite advantage for survival. Bugs can thrive on minute amounts of food and can hide, fly, and live in huge numbers in a small space.

Bugs produce important products such as honey, beeswax, and silk. It is difficult to imagine that scientists could initiate the study of genetics because of bugs! Even social scientists have successfully studied the behavioral and communication patterns of bees.

Our world could not exist without bugs. These small, ever-abundant creatures have an irreplaceable role in the environment. Their shapes, colors, movements, behaviors, and habits are amazing and inspiring.

Simple Butterfly

The Butterfly is a well-loved, beautiful and sometimes mysterious insect. From the regal yellow and black Monarch to the huge Owl Butterfly, these creatures have fascinated humans and have even provided chasing sport for playful dogs for centuries.

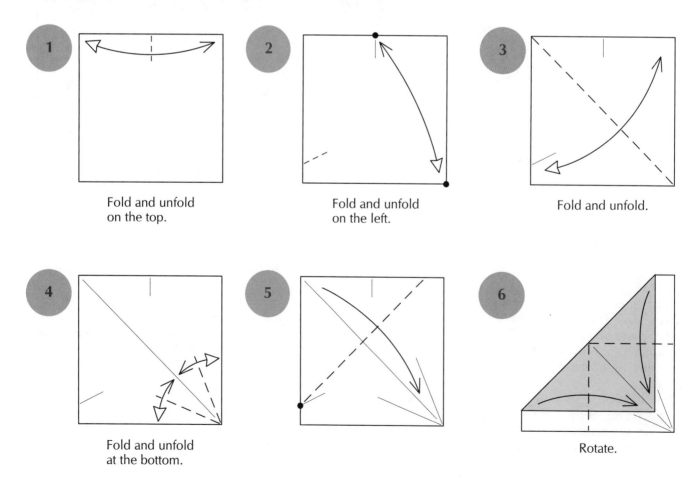

1 Fold and unfold on the top.

2 Fold and unfold on the left.

3 Fold and unfold.

4 Fold and unfold at the bottom.

5

6 Rotate.

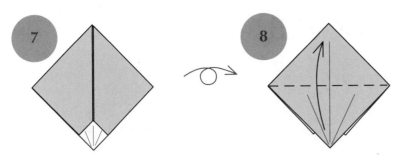

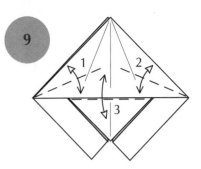

Fold the top layer up.

Fold and unfold the top layers in order.

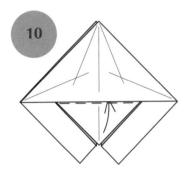

Tuck inside.

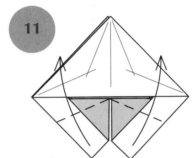

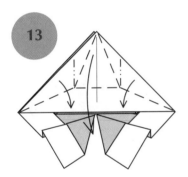

Fold along the creases.

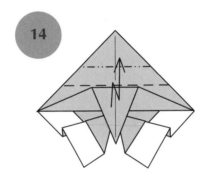

Pleat-fold.

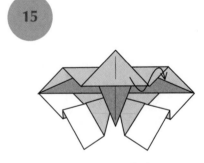

Tuck under the dark paper.

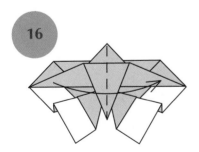

Fold in half.

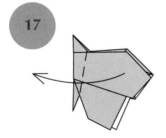

Repeat behind and spread.

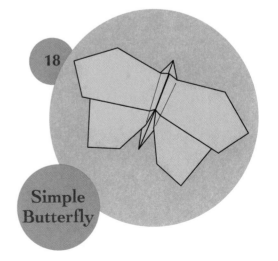

Simple Butterfly

Dragonfly

This exotic insect can usually be found around water. It has two pairs of transparent wings that span over its 1 to 5 inch body. These bugs can be any color which makes them even more intriguing but they are usually brightly colored with yellow, green, blue, or red spots or stripes that stand out.

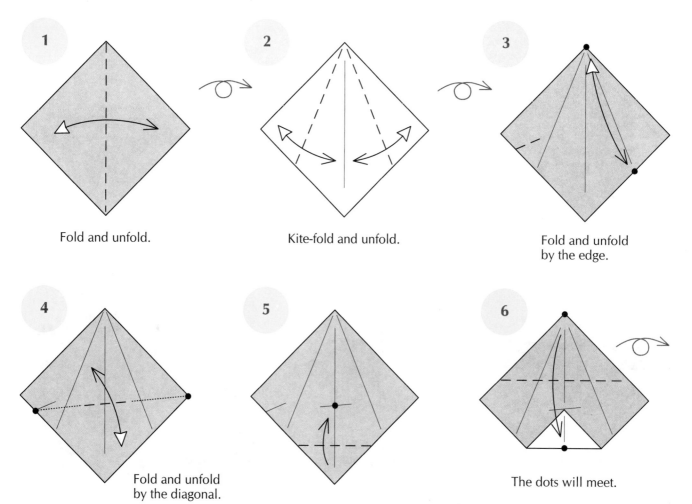

1 Fold and unfold.

2 Kite-fold and unfold.

3 Fold and unfold by the edge.

4 Fold and unfold by the diagonal.

5

6 The dots will meet.

7

8

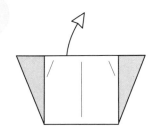

Unfold from behind.

9

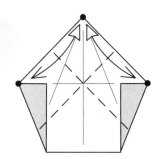

Fold and unfold.

10

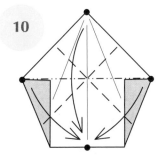

This is similar to the preliminary fold. The dots will meet.

11

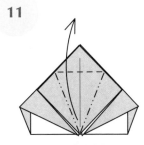

Petal-fold.

12

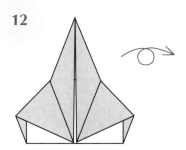

13

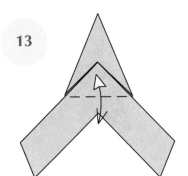

Fold and unfold.

14

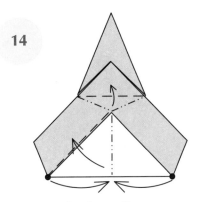

The dots will meet at the bottom.

15

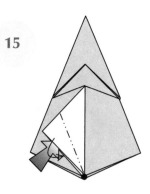

Reverse-fold.

16

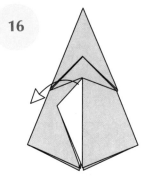

Pull out.

17

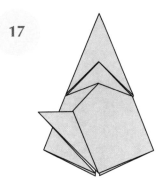

18

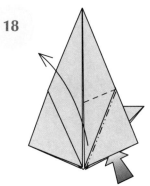

Squash-fold.

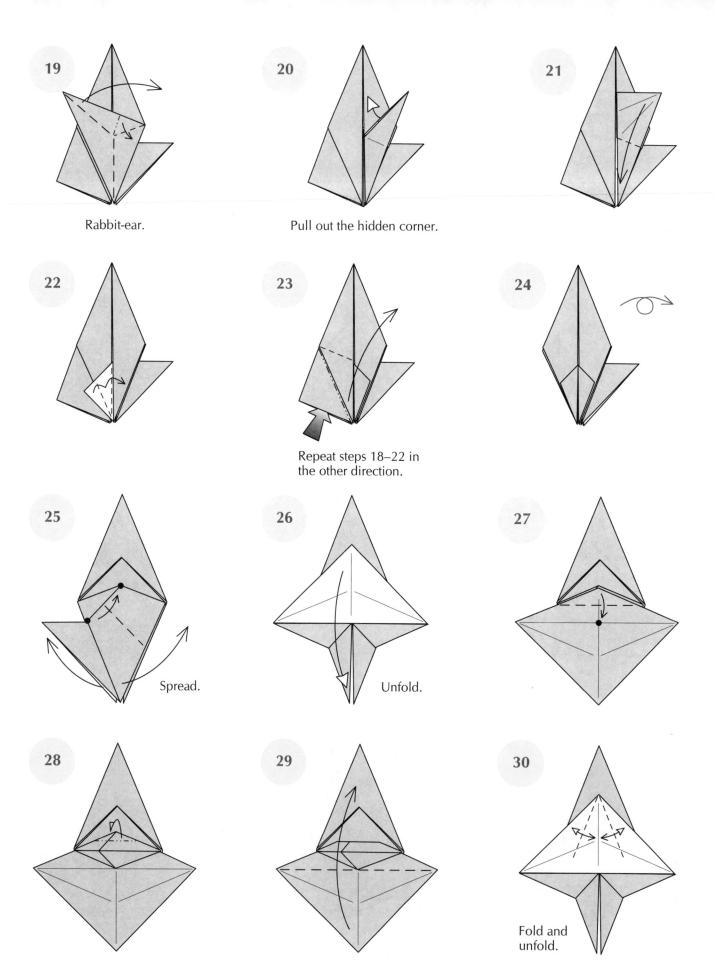

19 Rabbit-ear.

20 Pull out the hidden corner.

21

22

23 Repeat steps 18–22 in the other direction.

24

25 Spread.

26 Unfold.

27

28

29

30 Fold and unfold.

31

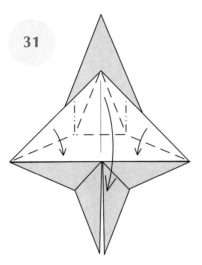

Fold along the creases.

32

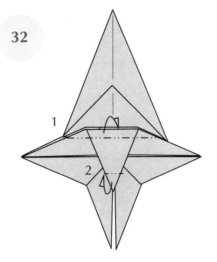

Fold behind along a hidden crease at 1.

33

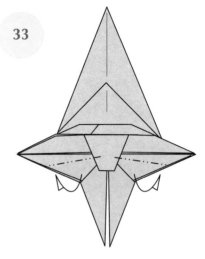

Slide the paper. This is similar to a reverse fold.

34

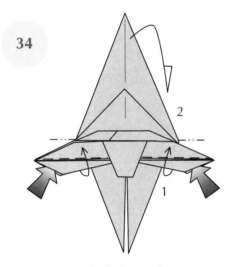

1. Unlock the top layer.
2. Fold behind.

35

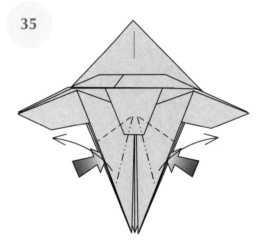

Squash folds.

36

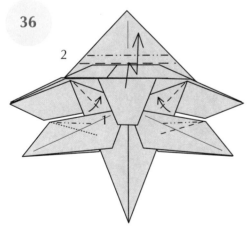

1. Fold on the top wing and on hidden layers of the lower wing.
2. Pleat-fold.

37

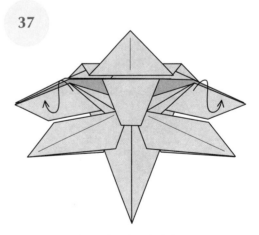

Tuck under the dark layer.

38

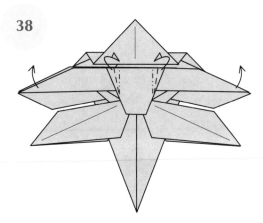

39

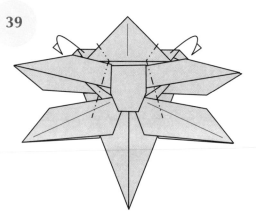

Mountain-fold on the head
and on hidden layers.

40

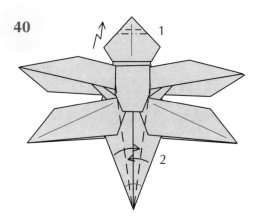

1. Pleat-fold.
2. Divide the tail in thirds.

41

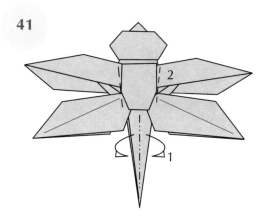

Shape the dragonfly.

42

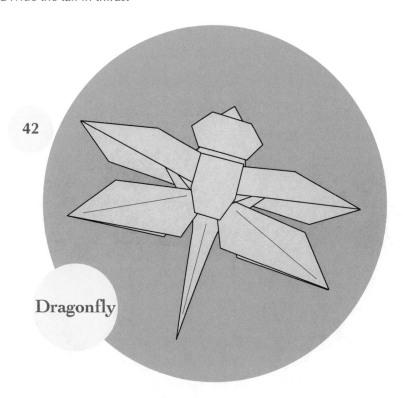

Dragonfly

Moth

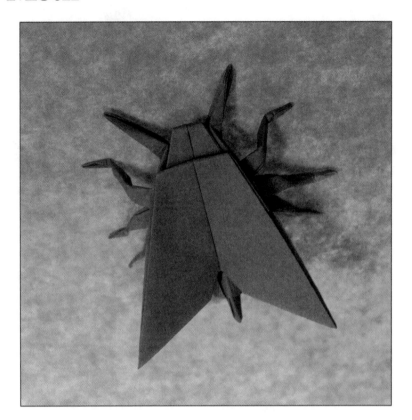

The Moth is a close relative of the Butterfly and often features a less complex design on its wings. Known in popular culture for gathering around flames and bright lights as well as being sneaky and voracious eaters of sweaters, the moth comes in many sizes, one of the largest being the Luna Moth.

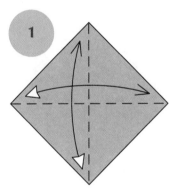

Fold and unfold.

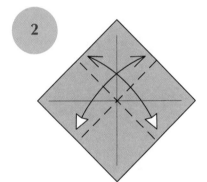

Fold and unfold.

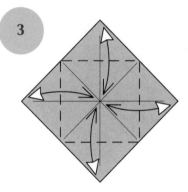

Fold to the center and unfold. Rotate.

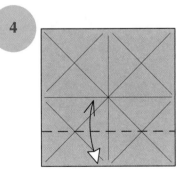

Fold and unfold. Rotate 90°.

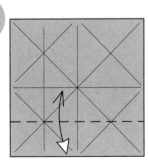

Repeat step 4 three times. Rotate.

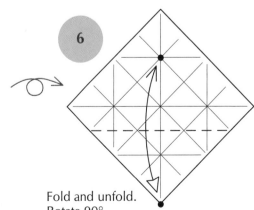

Fold and unfold. Rotate 90°.

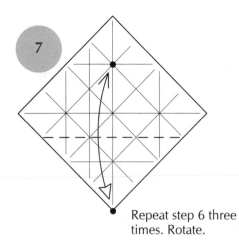

7 Repeat step 6 three times. Rotate.

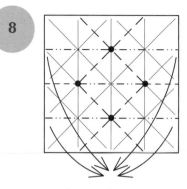

8 Push in at the dots and fold along the creases.

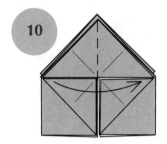

9 Repeat behind.

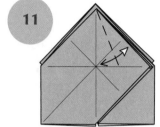

10

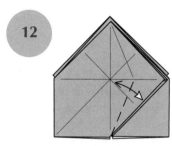

11 Fold and unfold the top flap.

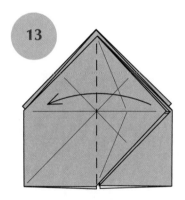

12 Fold and unfold the top flap.

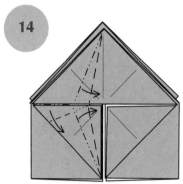

13

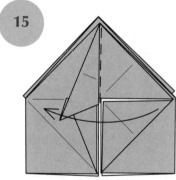

14 This is similar to a rabbit ear.

15 Repeat steps 10–14 on the right.

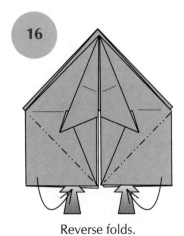

16 Reverse folds.

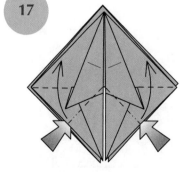

17 Crimp folds.

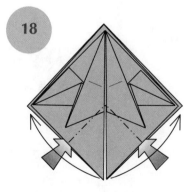

18 Reverse folds.

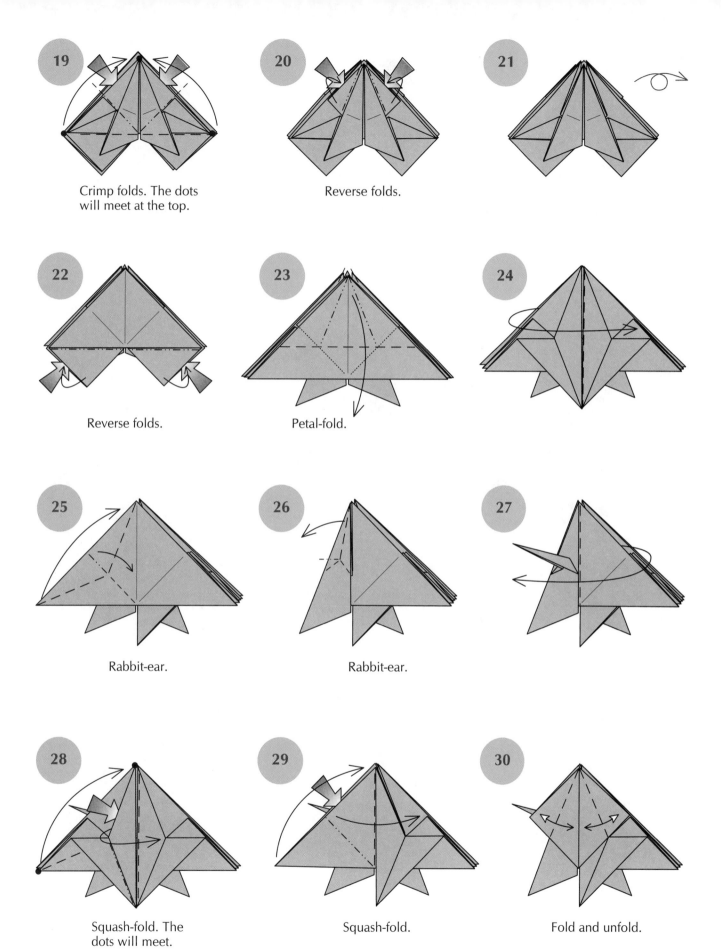

19 Crimp folds. The dots will meet at the top.

20 Reverse folds.

21

22 Reverse folds.

23 Petal-fold.

24

25 Rabbit-ear.

26 Rabbit-ear.

27

28 Squash-fold. The dots will meet.

29 Squash-fold.

30 Fold and unfold.

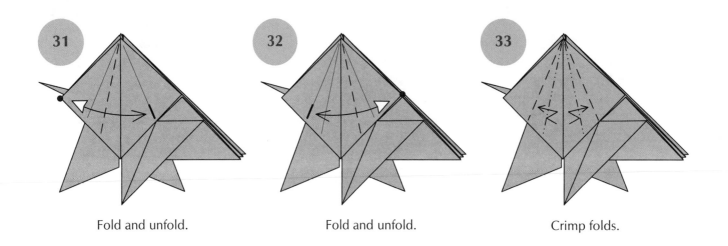

31 Fold and unfold.

32 Fold and unfold.

33 Crimp folds.

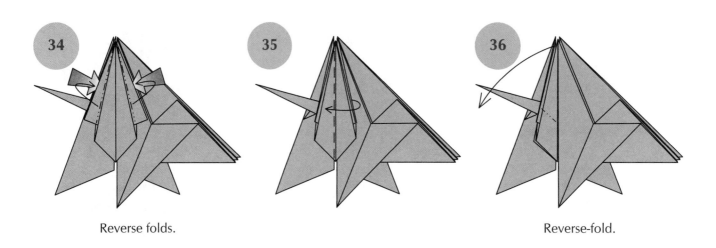

34 Reverse folds.

35

36 Reverse-fold.

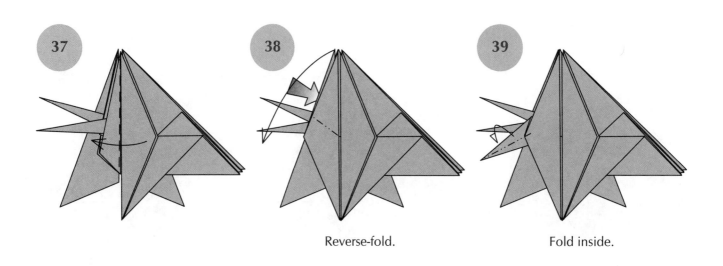

37

38 Reverse-fold.

39 Fold inside.

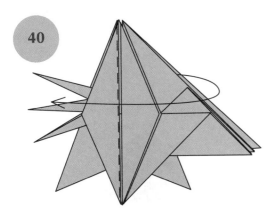

40

Repeat steps 24–39
on the right.

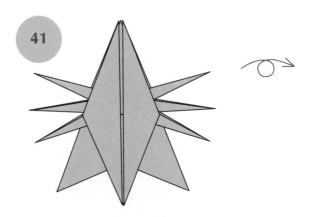

41

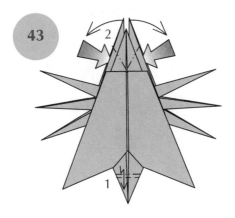

42

1. Fold behind.
2. Pleat-fold.

43

1. Pleat-fold.
2. Reverse folds.

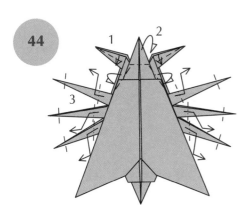

44

1. Thin the antennae, repeat behind.
2. Fold behind.
3. Shape the legs.

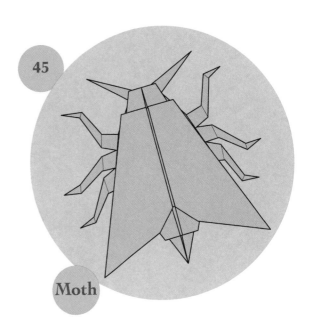

45

Moth

Fly

The Fly is one of approximately 85,000 different insects known as dipterans. These creatures can be found just about anywhere on earth, from sub-Arctic conditions to the serene environment of the high mountains. The fly has an unremitting pursuit for food and drink; however, flies are one of the most important parts of the food chain.

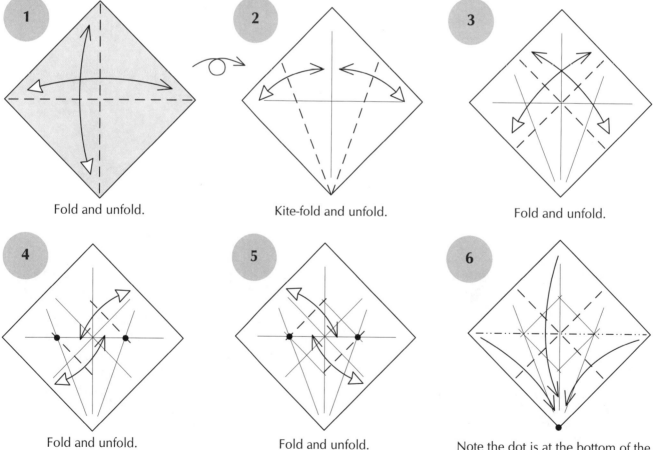

1 Fold and unfold.

2 Kite-fold and unfold.

3 Fold and unfold.

4 Fold and unfold.

5 Fold and unfold.

6 Note the dot is at the bottom of the kite-fold. Make a preliminary fold.

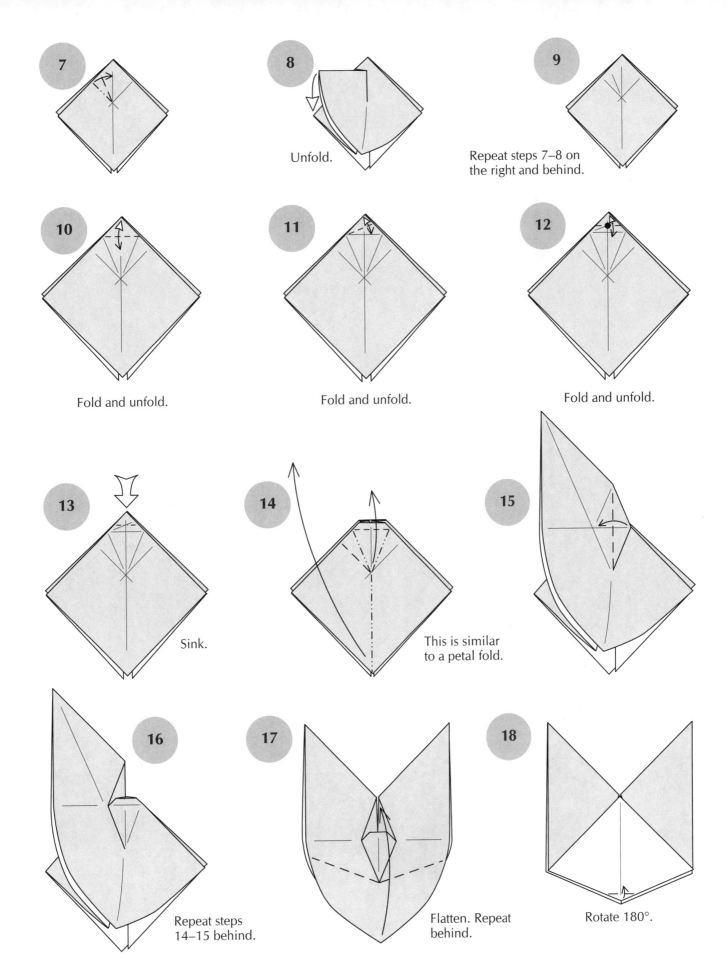

7

8

Unfold.

9

Repeat steps 7–8 on the right and behind.

10

Fold and unfold.

11

Fold and unfold.

12

Fold and unfold.

13

Sink.

14

This is similar to a petal fold.

15

16

Repeat steps 14–15 behind.

17

Flatten. Repeat behind.

18

Rotate 180°.

Fly 27

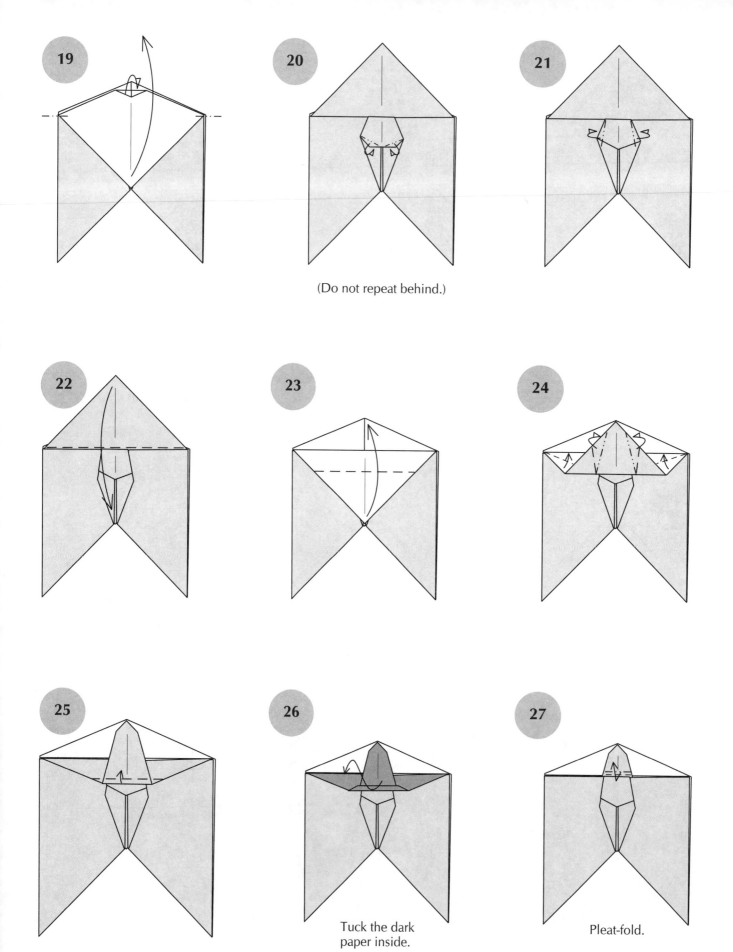

(Do not repeat behind.)

Tuck the dark
paper inside.

Pleat-fold.

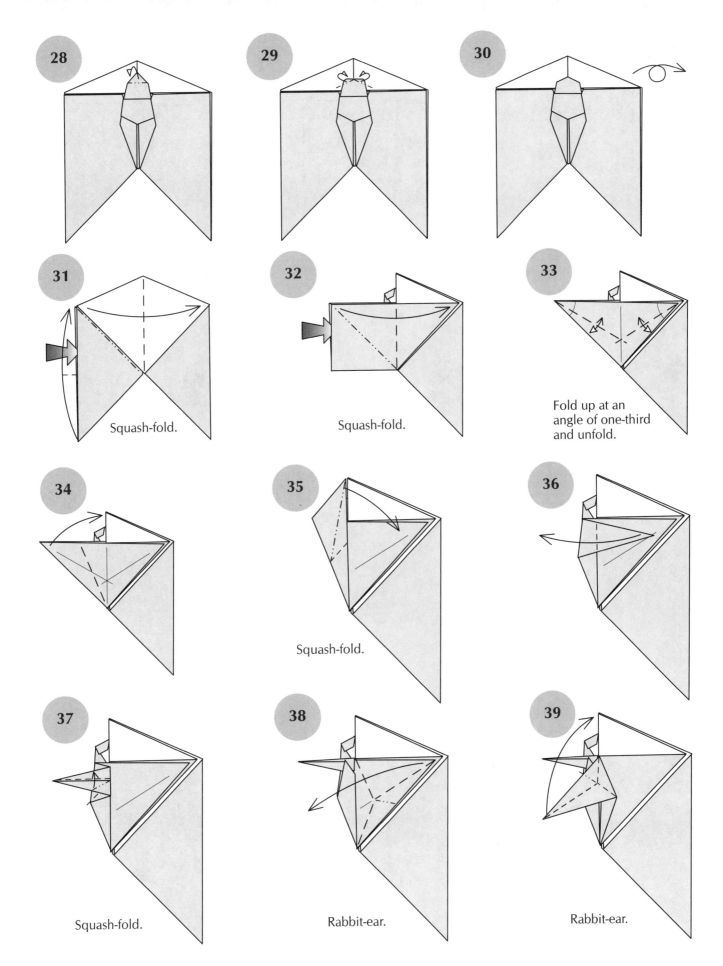

28

29

30

31

Squash-fold.

32

Squash-fold.

33

Fold up at an angle of one-third and unfold.

34

35

Squash-fold.

36

37

Squash-fold.

38

Rabbit-ear.

39

Rabbit-ear.

Fly 29

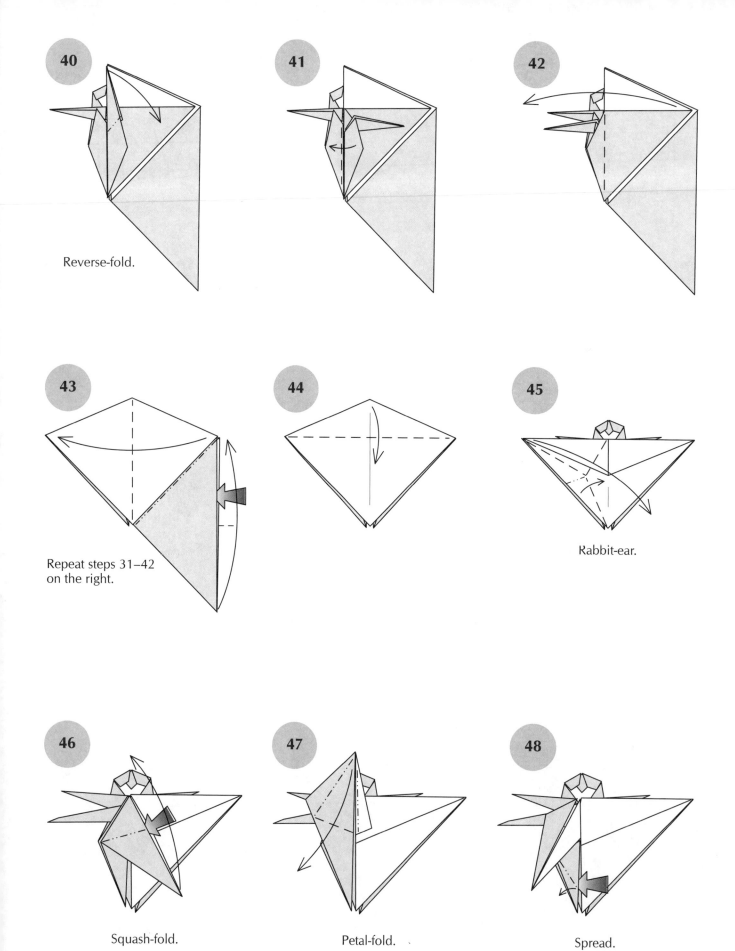

40 Reverse-fold.

41

42

43 Repeat steps 31–42 on the right.

44

45 Rabbit-ear.

46 Squash-fold.

47 Petal-fold.

48 Spread.

49

50

Repeat steps 45–49 on the right.

51

52

Tuck.

53

Spread the wings.

54

55

56

Fly

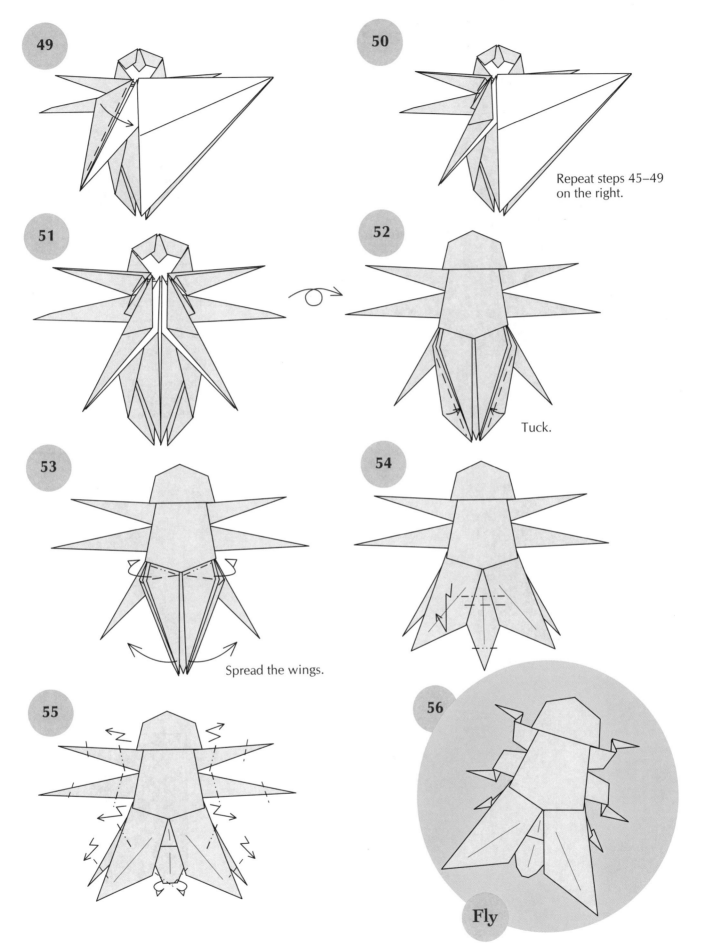

Praying Mantis

The Praying Mantis is a unique insect that appears to hold its "hands" in a praying position. Long and thin, it features a triangular head and sometimes is mistaken for a thin leaf. Unlike other insects, the Praying Mantis can turn its head and look behind itself.

1

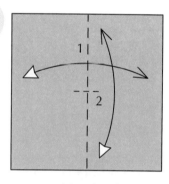

1. Fold and unfold.
2. Fold and unfold in the center.

2

Bring the edge to the center and crease at the top.

3

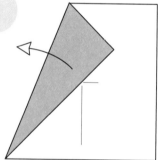

Unfold.

4

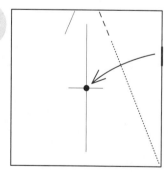

Repeat steps 2–3 on the right.

5

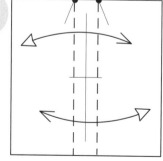

Fold and unfold.

6

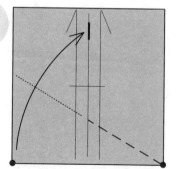

Bring the corner to the line. Crease on the right.

7

Unfold.

8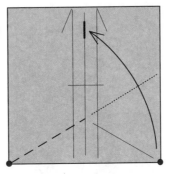

Repeat steps 6–7 in the other direction.

9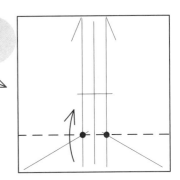

10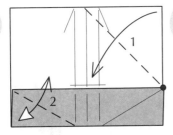

1. Fold beyond the center.
2. Fold and unfold along the crease.

11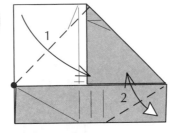

1. Overlap by the center.
2. Fold and unfold.

12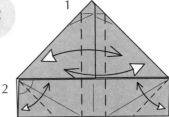

1. Fold and unfold along the creases at the bottom.
2. Fold and unfold.

13

Fold and unfold. Bisect the angles.

14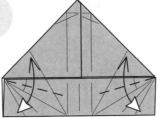

Fold and unfold. Bisect the angles.

15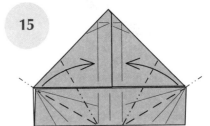

Make crimp folds along the creases.

16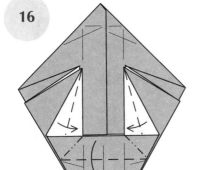

Petal-fold.

17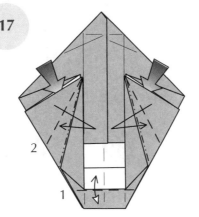

1. Fold and unfold all the layers.
2. Make crimp folds.

18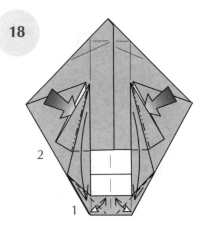

1. Fold and unfold all the layers.
2. Squash folds.

Praying Mantis 33

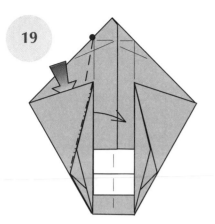

19

Reverse-fold.

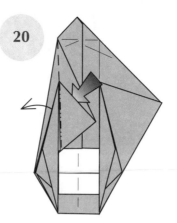

20

Reverse-fold.

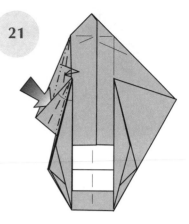

21

Reverse-fold twice
to divide the angle
in thirds.

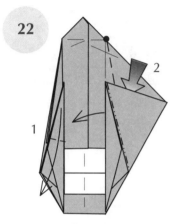

22

1. Fold down.
2. Repeat steps 19–22
   on the right.

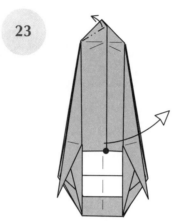

23

Pull out.

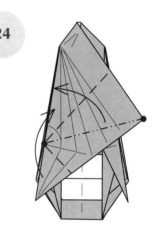

24

Bisect the angle
at the left dot.

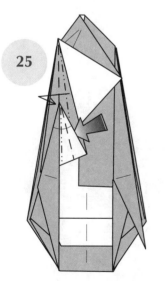

25

Make two reverse folds.
Divide the angle in thirds.

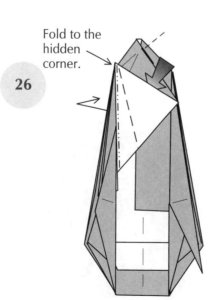

26

Fold to the
hidden
corner.

Make two reverse folds. The
bold line will be vertical and
lie as it was in step 23.

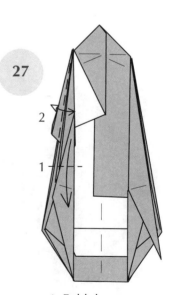

27

1. Fold down.
2. Fold and unfold.

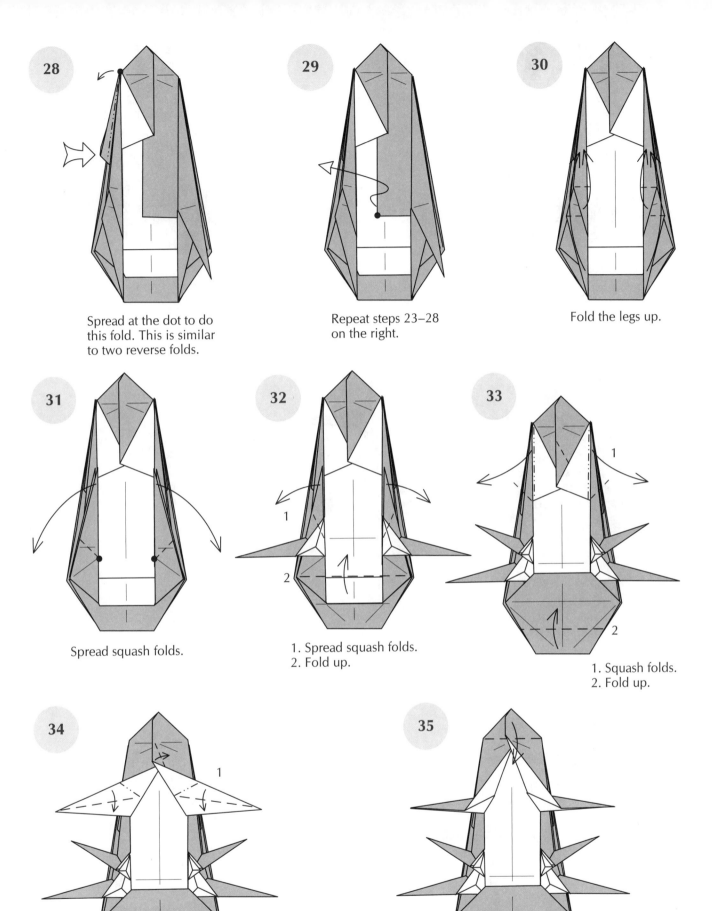

28

Spread at the dot to do this fold. This is similar to two reverse folds.

29

Repeat steps 23–28 on the right.

30

Fold the legs up.

31

Spread squash folds.

32

1. Spread squash folds.
2. Fold up.

33

1. Squash folds.
2. Fold up.

34

1. Squash folds.
2. Reverse folds.

35

36

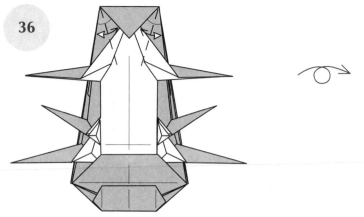

Fold and unfold.

37

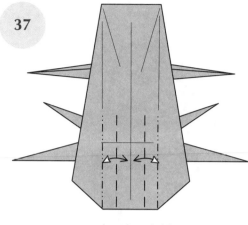

Make pleat folds
on the bottom.

38

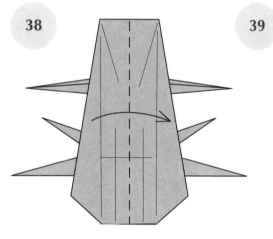

Fold in half.

39

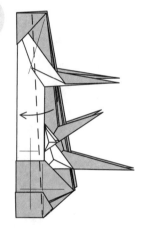

Fold in half. Repeat
behind and rotate.

40

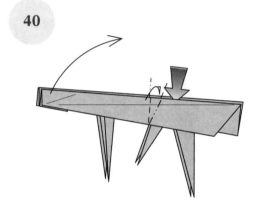

Crimp-fold.

41

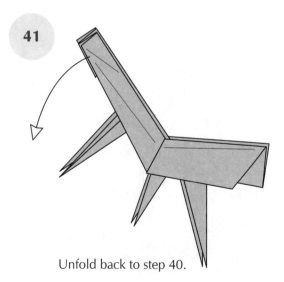

Unfold back to step 40.

42

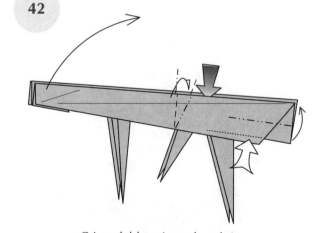

Crimp-fold again and push in
by the wings for a reverse fold.

43

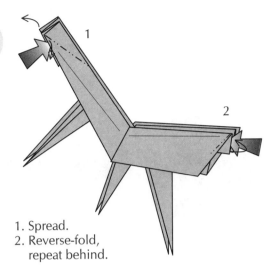

1. Spread.
2. Reverse-fold, repeat behind.

44

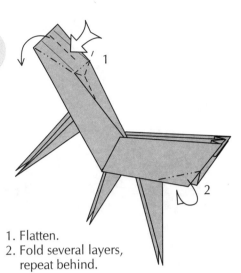

1. Flatten.
2. Fold several layers, repeat behind.

45

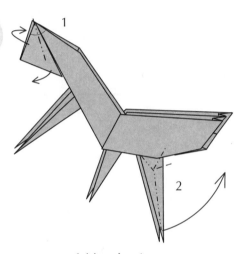

1. Reverse-fold and swing out.
2. Double-rabbit-ear, repeat behind.

46

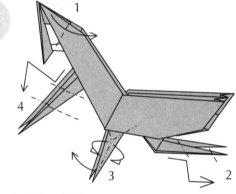

1. Valley-fold.
2. Reverse-folds.
3. Thin the legs.
4. Reverse-folds.
Repeat behind at the legs.

47

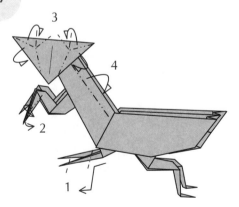

1. Bend the legs.
2. Spread and curl the arms.
3. Shape the antennae.
4. Thin the body.
Repeat behind at 1, 2, and 4.

48

Praying Mantis

Hornet

The Hornet is part of the Wasp family, and like wasps and many bees, is known in popular culture for its sting. It has come to be represented by superheroes and sports mascots.

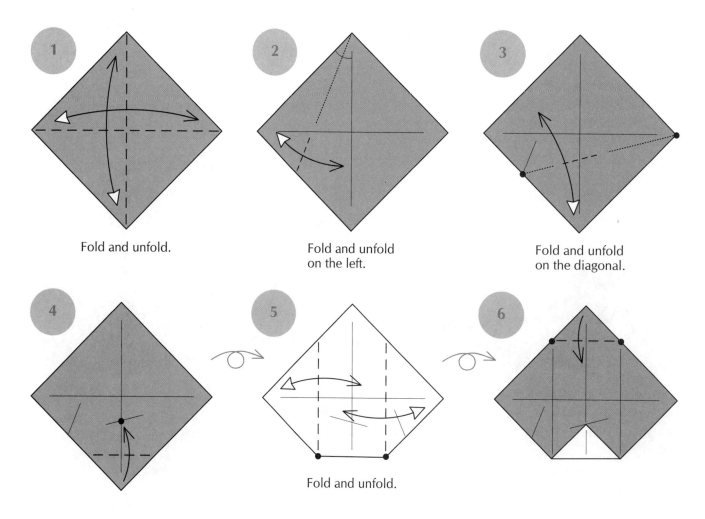

1 Fold and unfold.

2 Fold and unfold on the left.

3 Fold and unfold on the diagonal.

4

5 Fold and unfold.

6

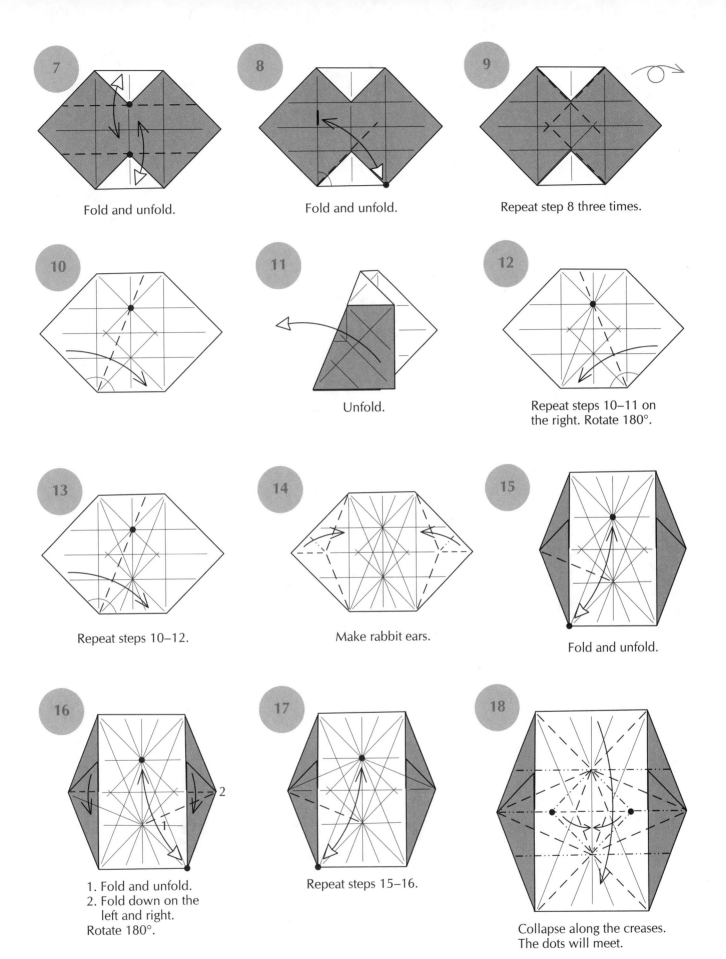

7 Fold and unfold.

8 Fold and unfold.

9 Repeat step 8 three times.

10

11 Unfold.

12 Repeat steps 10–11 on the right. Rotate 180°.

13 Repeat steps 10–12.

14 Make rabbit ears.

15 Fold and unfold.

16
1. Fold and unfold.
2. Fold down on the left and right.
Rotate 180°.

17 Repeat steps 15–16.

18 Collapse along the creases. The dots will meet.

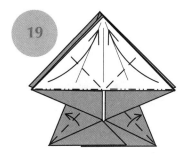

19

Squash folds.
Repeat behind.

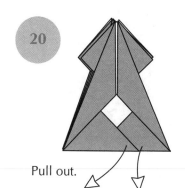

20

Pull out.

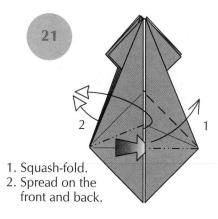

21

1. Squash-fold.
2. Spread on the
   front and back.

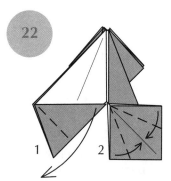

22

1. Outside-reverse-fold.
2. Kite-fold.

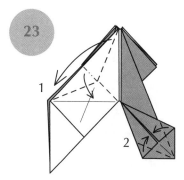

23

1. This is similar to a rabbit
   ear, repeat behind.
2. Kite-fold.

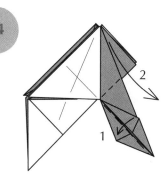

24

1. Fold in half.
2. Repeat behind.

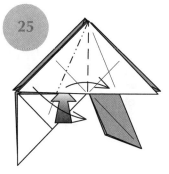

25

Squash-fold.
Repeat behind.

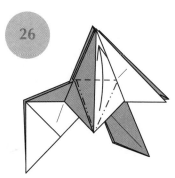

26

This is similar to a petal
fold. Repeat behind.

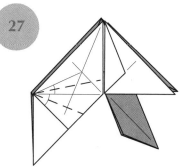

27

Fold and unfold all the
layers. Bisect the angles.

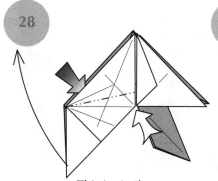

28

This is similar to a
reverse fold and sink.

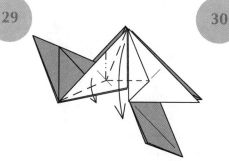

29

Repeat behind.

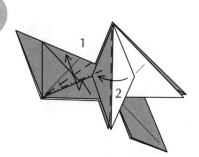

30

1. Crimp-fold.
2. Repeat behind.

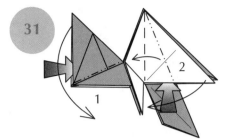

31

1. Reverse-fold.
2. Squash-fold, repeat behind.

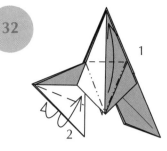

32

1. Petal-fold, repeat behind.
2. Outside-reverse-fold.

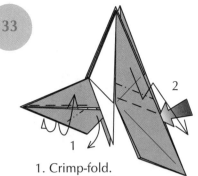

33

1. Crimp-fold.
2. This is similar to a crimp fold and sink.

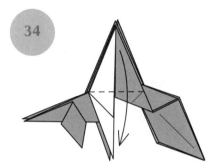

34

Repeat behind.

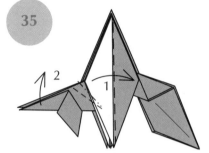

35

1. Repeat behind.
2. Crimp-fold.

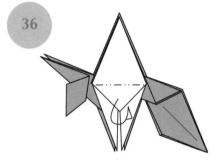

36

Fold inside, repeat behind.

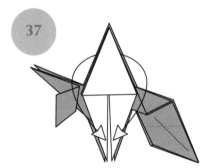

37

This is similar to the double-unwrap-fold. Repeat behind.

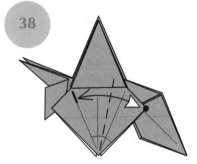

38

Fold and unfold. Repeat behind.

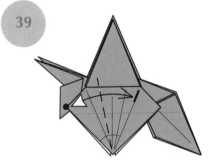

39

Fold and unfold. Repeat behind.

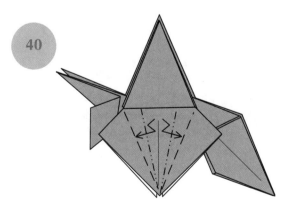

40

Crimp folds. Repeat behind.

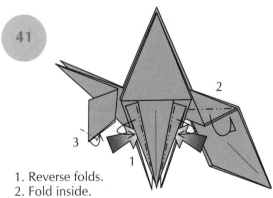

41

1. Reverse folds.
2. Fold inside.
3. Reverse-fold. Repeat behind.

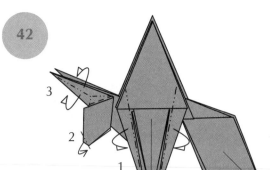

42

1. Fold inside.
2. Reverse-fold.
3. Thin the antennae.
Repeat behind.

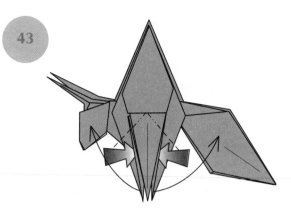

43

Reverse folds.
Repeat behind.

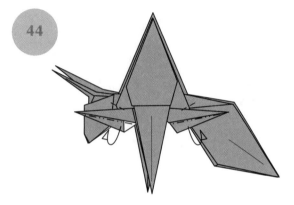

44

Reverse folds.
Repeat behind.

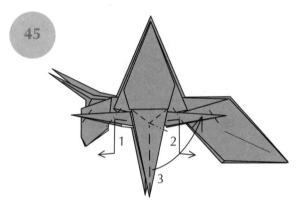

45

1. Reverse folds.
2. Reverse folds.
3. Rabbit-ear.
Repeat behind.

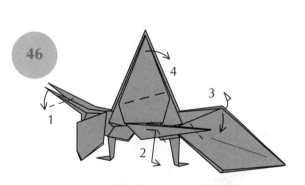

46

1. Bend the antennae.
2. Outside-reverse folds.
3. Spread the tail.
4. Spread the wings.
Repeat behind.

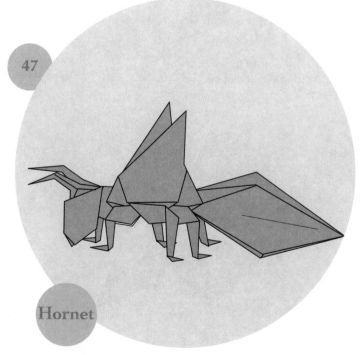

47

Hornet

Ant

The Ant is a very social insect and many varieties of ants utilize very specific social structures and languages to communicate within their group. Some do a lot of heavy lifting work and some behave like armies, capable of eating just about anything organic in their path.

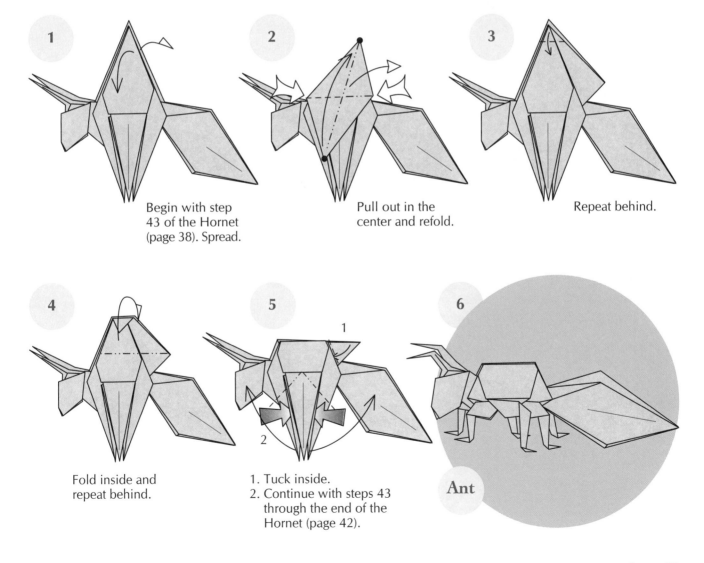

1 Begin with step 43 of the Hornet (page 38). Spread.

2 Pull out in the center and refold.

3 Repeat behind.

4 Fold inside and repeat behind.

5
1. Tuck inside.
2. Continue with steps 43 through the end of the Hornet (page 42).

6 Ant

Wasp

There are over 20,000 species of wasps. These stinging insects are thin between the thorax and abdomen. The adults feed on nectar while the larvae feed on insects. The most familiar wasps are yellow jackets and hornets.

1

Fold and unfold.

2

Fold and unfold on the left.

3

Fold and unfold on the diagonal.

4

5

Fold and unfold.

6

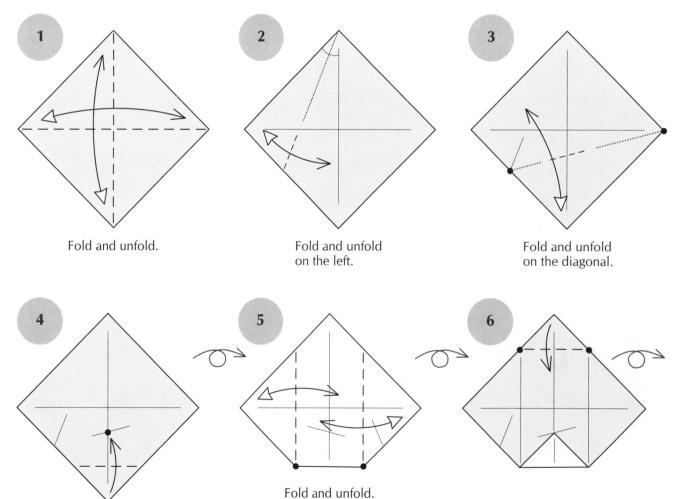

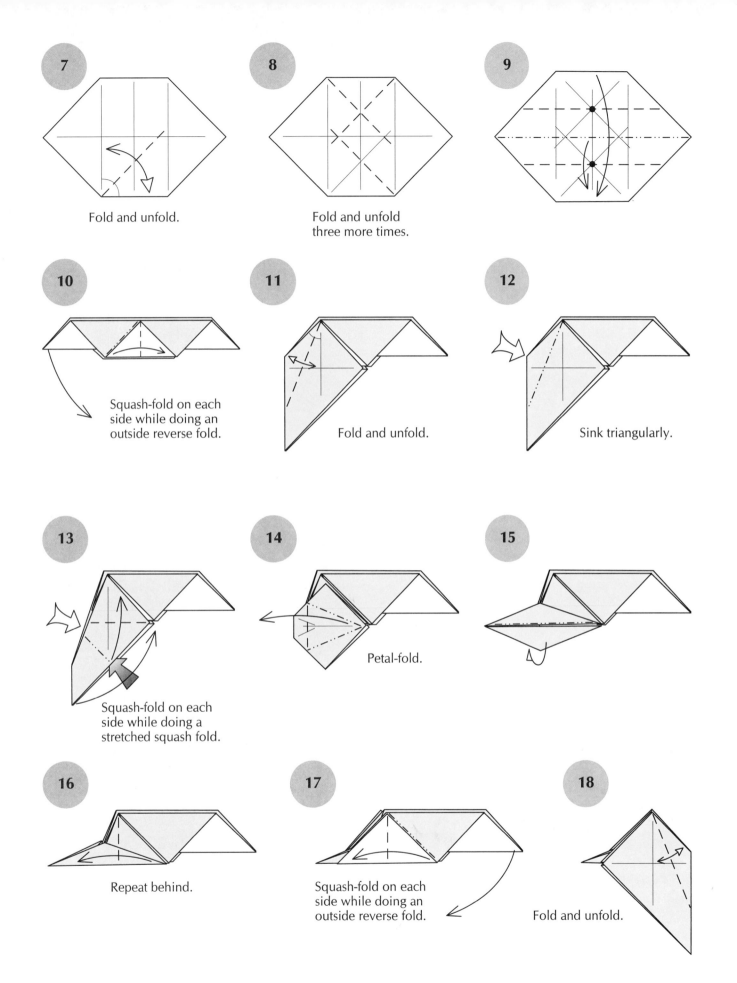

7

Fold and unfold.

8

Fold and unfold
three more times.

9

10

Squash-fold on each
side while doing an
outside reverse fold.

11

Fold and unfold.

12

Sink triangularly.

13

Squash-fold on each
side while doing a
stretched squash fold.

14

Petal-fold.

15

16

Repeat behind.

17

Squash-fold on each
side while doing an
outside reverse fold.

18

Fold and unfold.

Wasp 45

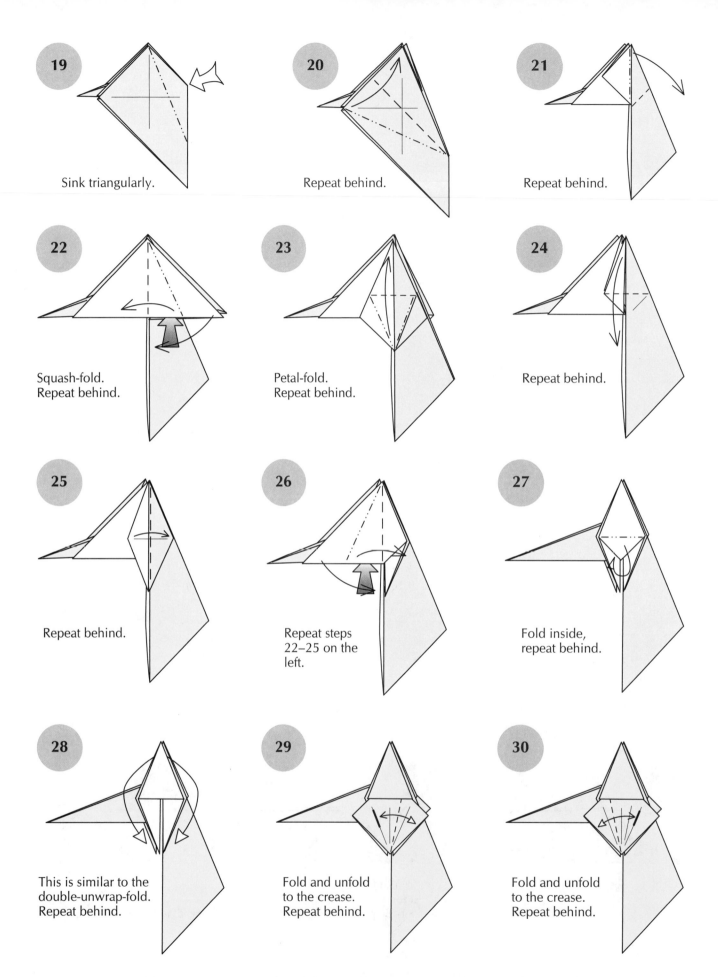

19 Sink triangularly.

20 Repeat behind.

21 Repeat behind.

22 Squash-fold. Repeat behind.

23 Petal-fold. Repeat behind.

24 Repeat behind.

25 Repeat behind.

26 Repeat steps 22–25 on the left.

27 Fold inside, repeat behind.

28 This is similar to the double-unwrap-fold. Repeat behind.

29 Fold and unfold to the crease. Repeat behind.

30 Fold and unfold to the crease. Repeat behind.

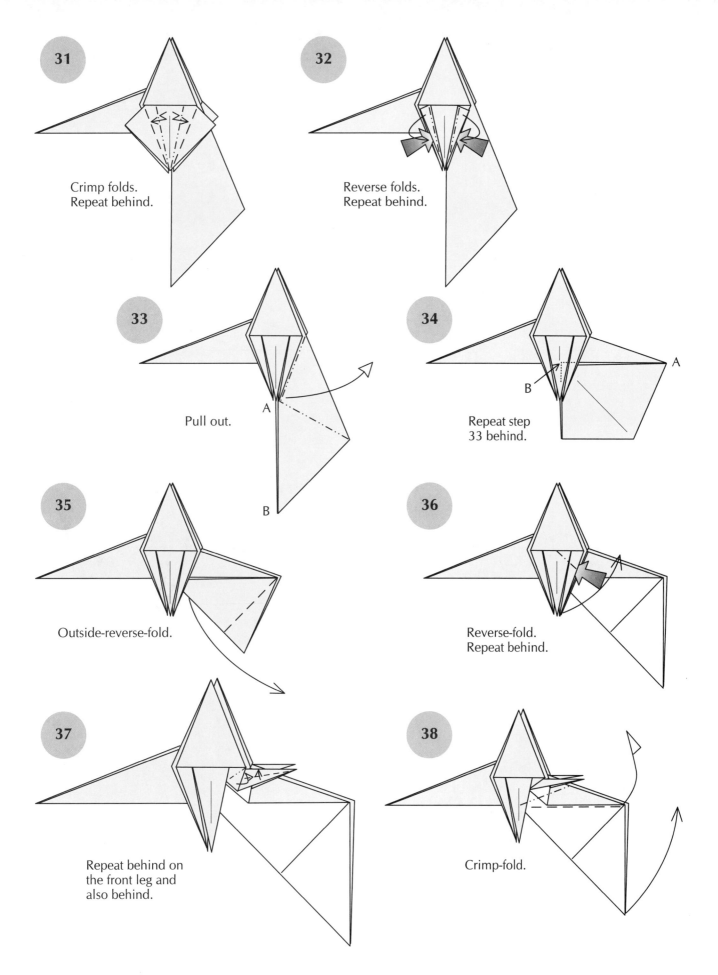

31 Crimp folds. Repeat behind.

32 Reverse folds. Repeat behind.

33 Pull out.

A

B

34 Repeat step 33 behind.

A

B

35 Outside-reverse-fold.

36 Reverse-fold. Repeat behind.

37 Repeat behind on the front leg and also behind.

38 Crimp-fold.

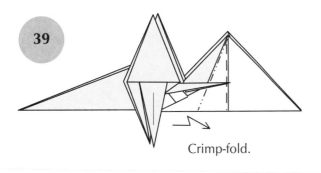

39

Crimp-fold.

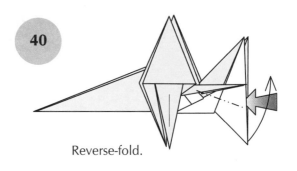

40

Reverse-fold.

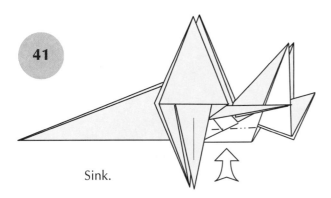

41

Sink.

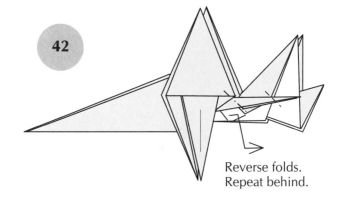

42

Reverse folds.
Repeat behind.

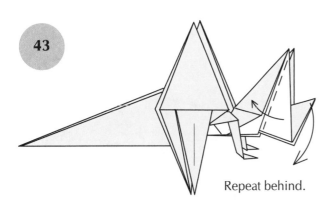

43

Repeat behind.

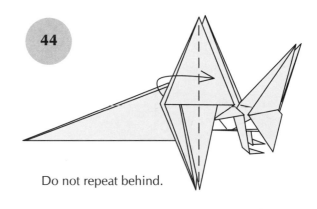

44

Do not repeat behind.

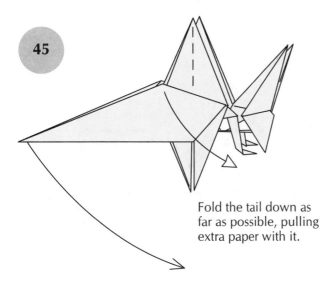

45

Fold the tail down as
far as possible, pulling
extra paper with it.

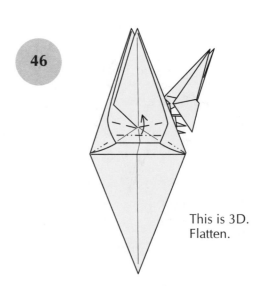

46

This is 3D.
Flatten.

47

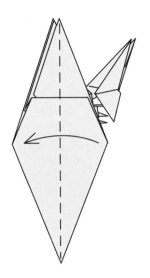

48

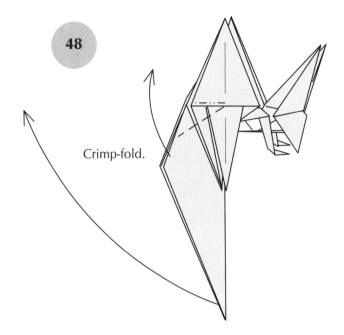

Crimp-fold.

49

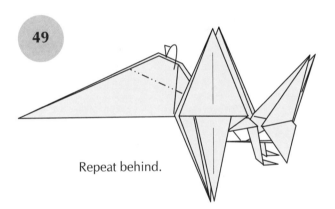

Repeat behind.

50

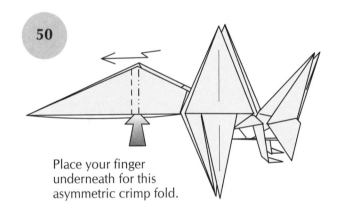

Place your finger underneath for this asymmetric crimp fold.

51

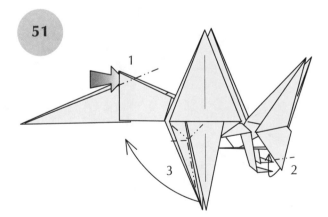

1. Reverse-fold.
2. Reverse-fold.
3. Double-rabbit-ear the legs, repeat behind.

52

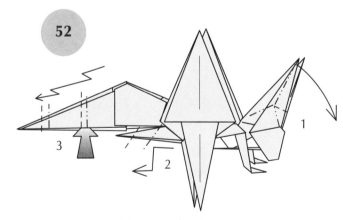

1. Double-rabbit-ear the antennae.
2. Reverse-fold the legs.
3. Crimp-fold the tail.
Repeat behind.

Wasp 49

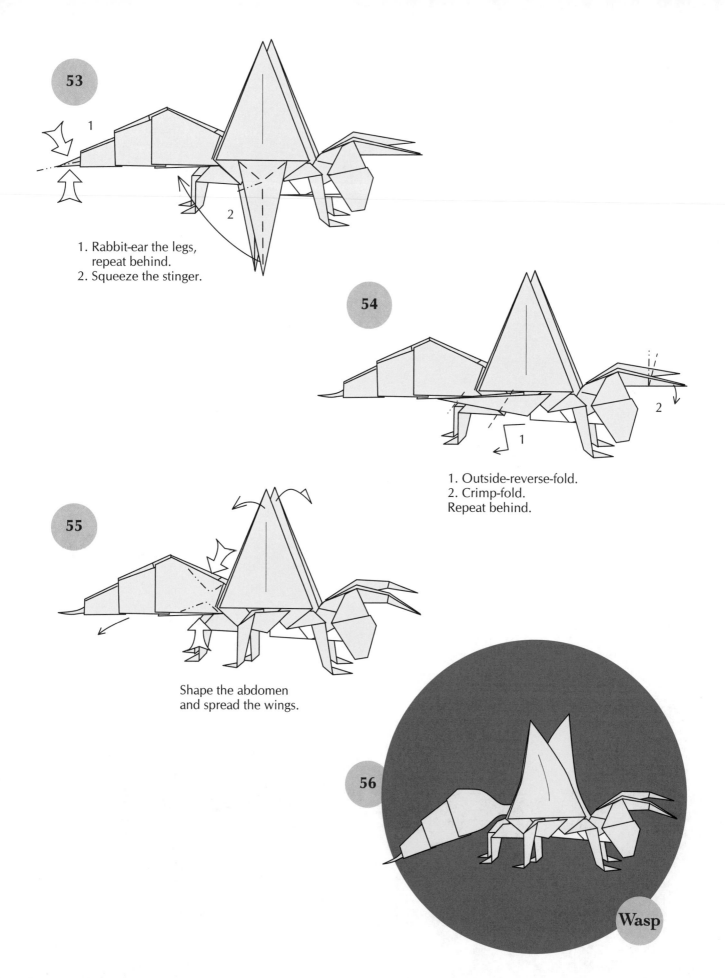

53

1. Rabbit-ear the legs, repeat behind.
2. Squeeze the stinger.

54

1. Outside-reverse-fold.
2. Crimp-fold.
Repeat behind.

55

Shape the abdomen and spread the wings.

56

Wasp

Grasshopper

The Grasshopper is known for its jumping behavior, though it can fly. Many people recall chasing grasshoppers on hot Spring or Summer days. Sometimes large groups of Grasshoppers fly together, creating a swarm.

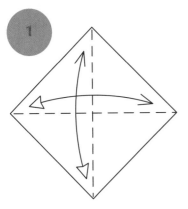

Fold and unfold.

Crease lightly.

Fold and unfold.

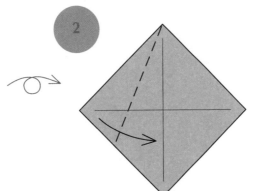

1. Fold to the dot.
2. Unfold.

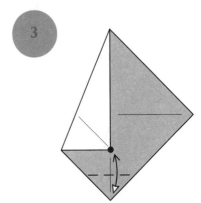

1. Fold and unfold.
2. Fold and unfold.
3. Unfold.

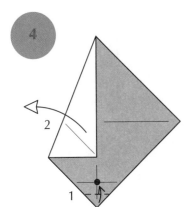

Pleat folds. Mountain-fold along the creases.

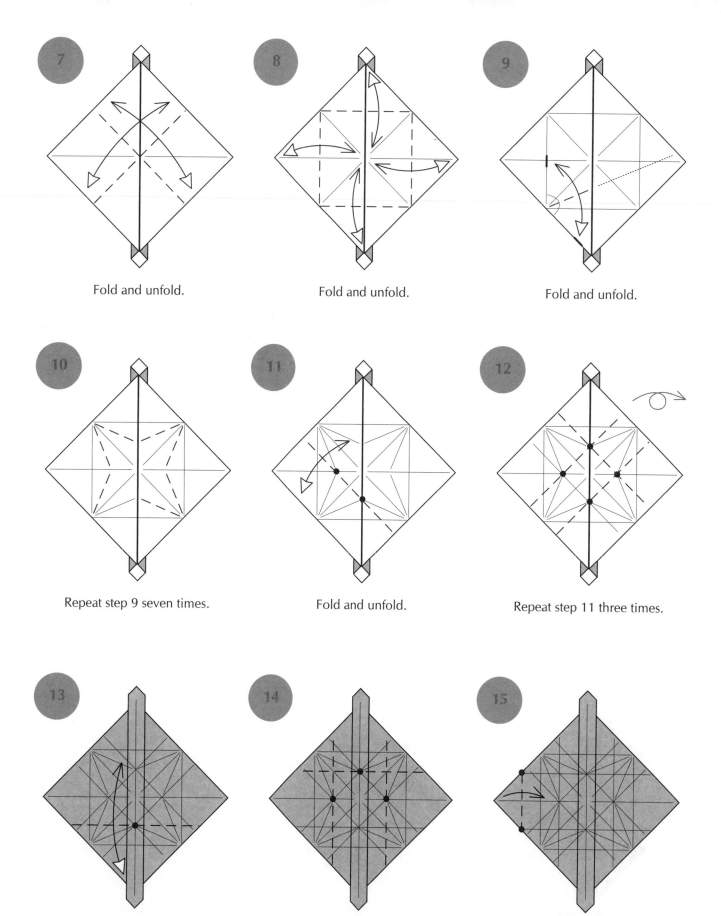

7 Fold and unfold.

8 Fold and unfold.

9 Fold and unfold.

10 Repeat step 9 seven times.

11 Fold and unfold.

12 Repeat step 11 three times.

13 Fold and unfold.

14 Repeat step 13 three times.

15

16

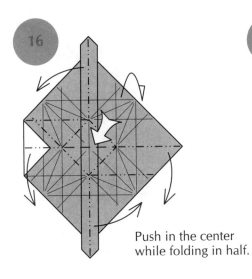

Push in the center
while folding in half.

17

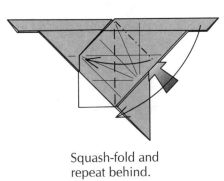

Squash-fold and
repeat behind.

18

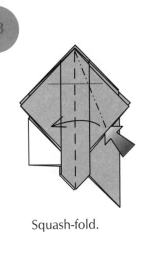

Squash-fold.

19

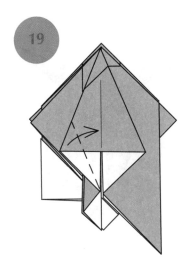

20

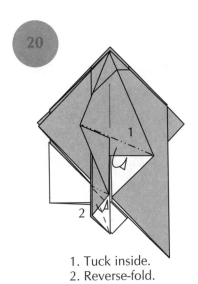

1. Tuck inside.
2. Reverse-fold.

21

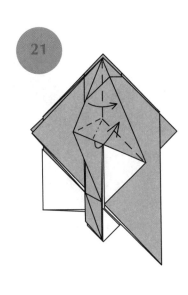

22

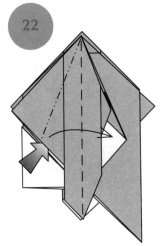

Repeat steps
18–21 on the left.

23

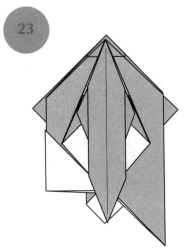

Repeat steps
18–22 behind.

24

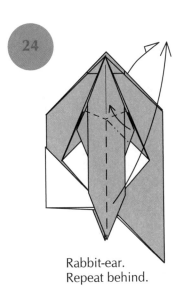

Rabbit-ear.
Repeat behind.

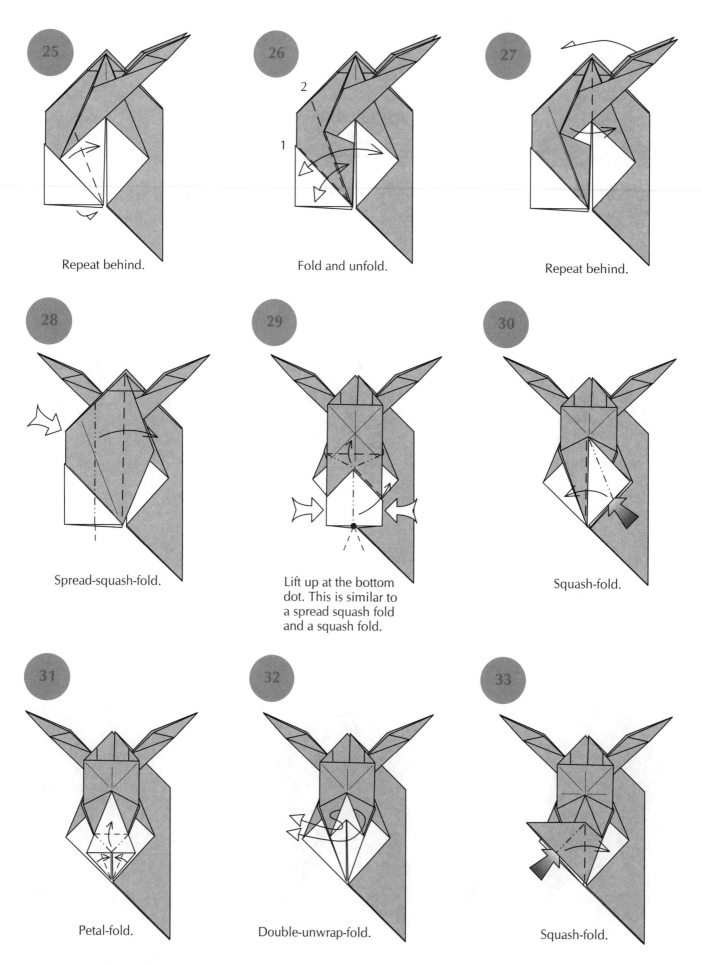

25

Repeat behind.

26

2

1

Fold and unfold.

27

Repeat behind.

28

Spread-squash-fold.

29

Lift up at the bottom dot. This is similar to a spread squash fold and a squash fold.

30

Squash-fold.

31

Petal-fold.

32

Double-unwrap-fold.

33

Squash-fold.

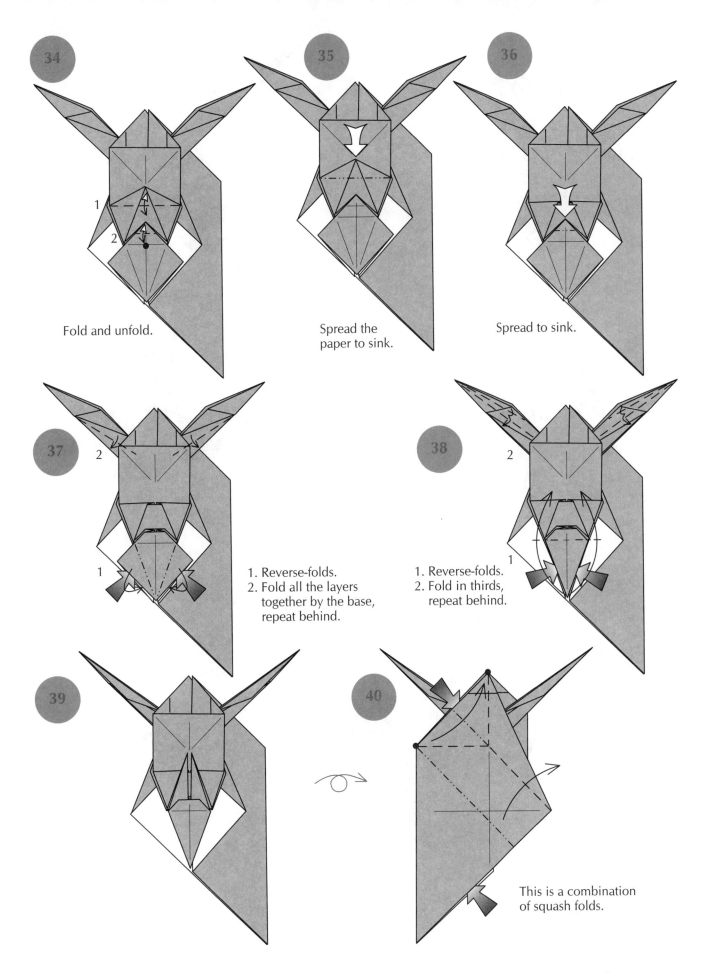

34 Fold and unfold.

35 Spread the paper to sink.

36 Spread to sink.

37
1. Reverse-folds.
2. Fold all the layers together by the base, repeat behind.

38
1. Reverse-folds.
2. Fold in thirds, repeat behind.

39

40 This is a combination of squash folds.

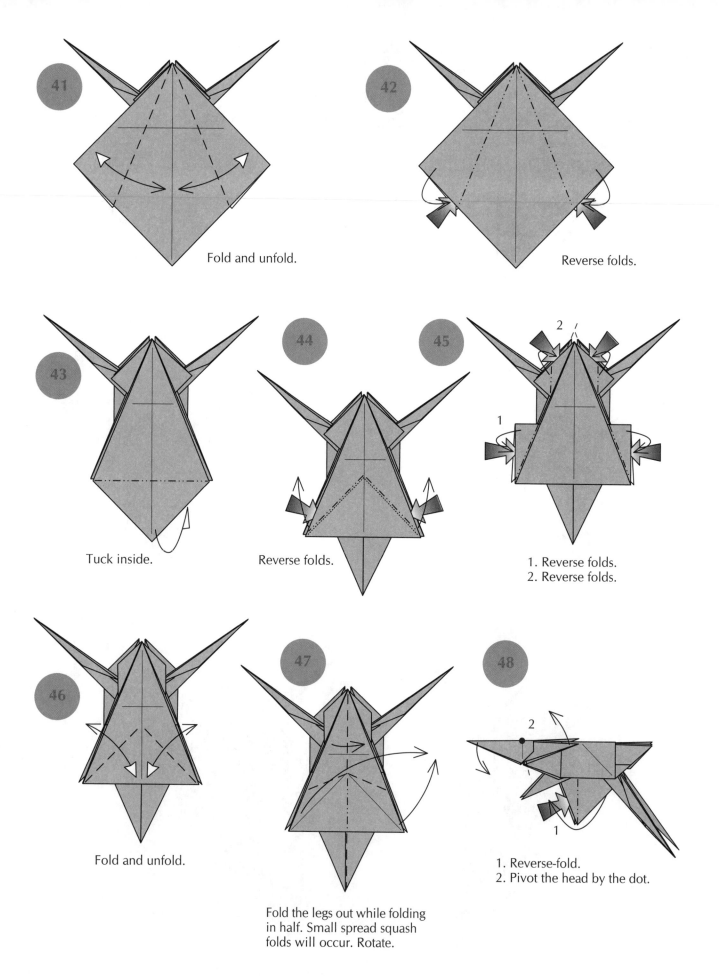

41 Fold and unfold.

42 Reverse folds.

43 Tuck inside.

44 Reverse folds.

45
1. Reverse folds.
2. Reverse folds.

46 Fold and unfold.

47 Fold the legs out while folding in half. Small spread squash folds will occur. Rotate.

48
1. Reverse-fold.
2. Pivot the head by the dot.

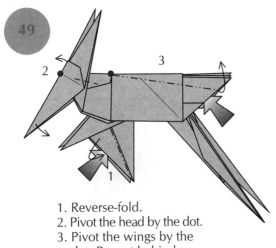

49

1. Reverse-fold.
2. Pivot the head by the dot.
3. Pivot the wings by the
   dot. Repeat behind.

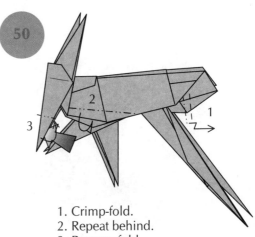

50

1. Crimp-fold.
2. Repeat behind.
3. Reverse-fold.

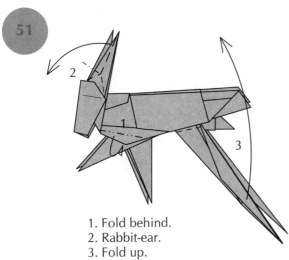

51

1. Fold behind.
2. Rabbit-ear.
3. Fold up.
Repeat behind.

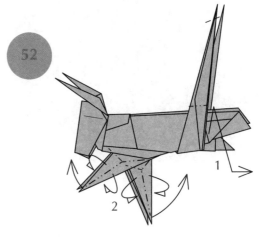

52

1. Reverse folds.
2. Thin the legs.
Repeat behind.

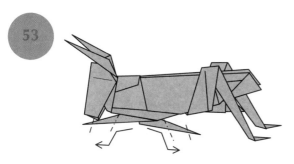

53

Bend the legs. Repeat behind.

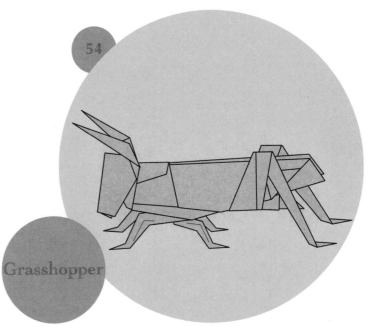

54

Grasshopper

Earwig

Earwigs are small insects that have large membranous hindwings that lie hidden under short, leathery forewings. The earwig varies from 5 to 50 millimeters in length and is flat, slender, and dark colored. This nocturnal insect is usually herbivorous. Several species can fire a foul-smelling liquid for distances up to 10 centimeters.

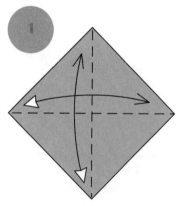

Fold and unfold.

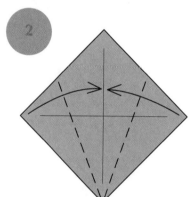

Kite-fold.

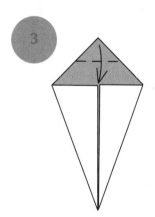

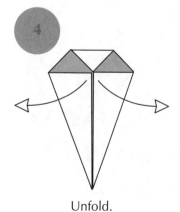

Unfold.

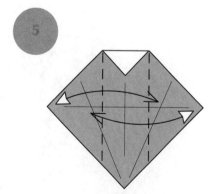

Fold and unfold.

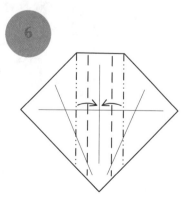

Pleat folds.

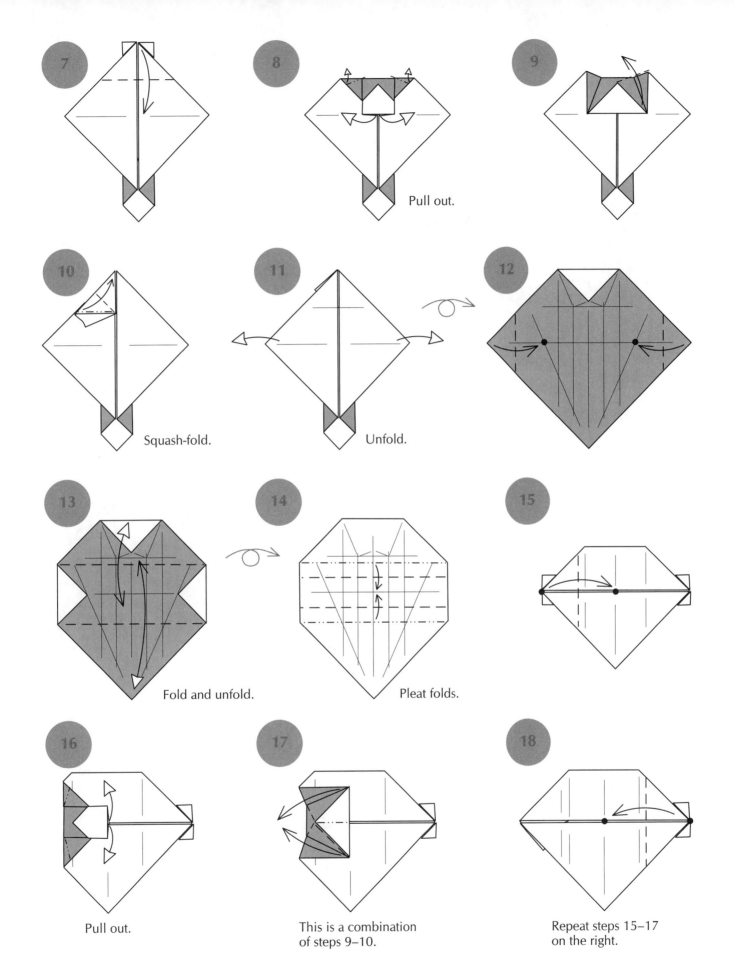

7

8 Pull out.

9

10 Squash-fold.

11 Unfold.

12

13 Fold and unfold.

14 Pleat folds.

15

16 Pull out.

17 This is a combination of steps 9–10.

18 Repeat steps 15–17 on the right.

Earwig 59

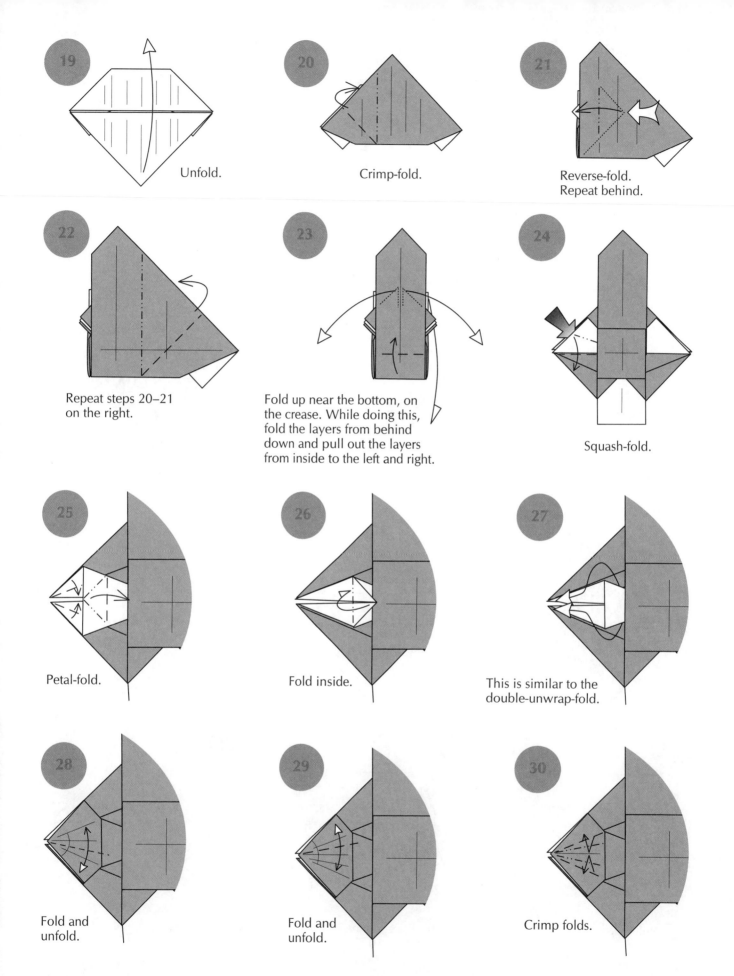

19 Unfold.

20 Crimp-fold.

21 Reverse-fold. Repeat behind.

22 Repeat steps 20–21 on the right.

23 Fold up near the bottom, on the crease. While doing this, fold the layers from behind down and pull out the layers from inside to the left and right.

24 Squash-fold.

25 Petal-fold.

26 Fold inside.

27 This is similar to the double-unwrap-fold.

28 Fold and unfold.

29 Fold and unfold.

30 Crimp folds.

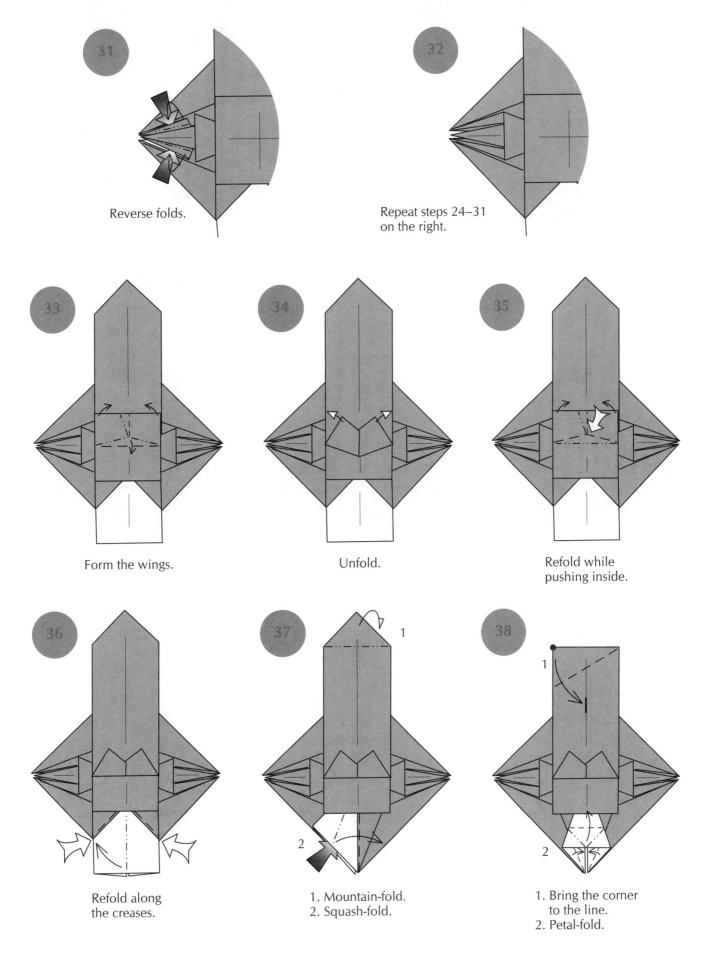

31 Reverse folds.

32 Repeat steps 24–31 on the right.

33 Form the wings.

34 Unfold.

35 Refold while pushing inside.

36 Refold along the creases.

37 1. Mountain-fold.
2. Squash-fold.

38 1. Bring the corner to the line.
2. Petal-fold.

Earwig 61

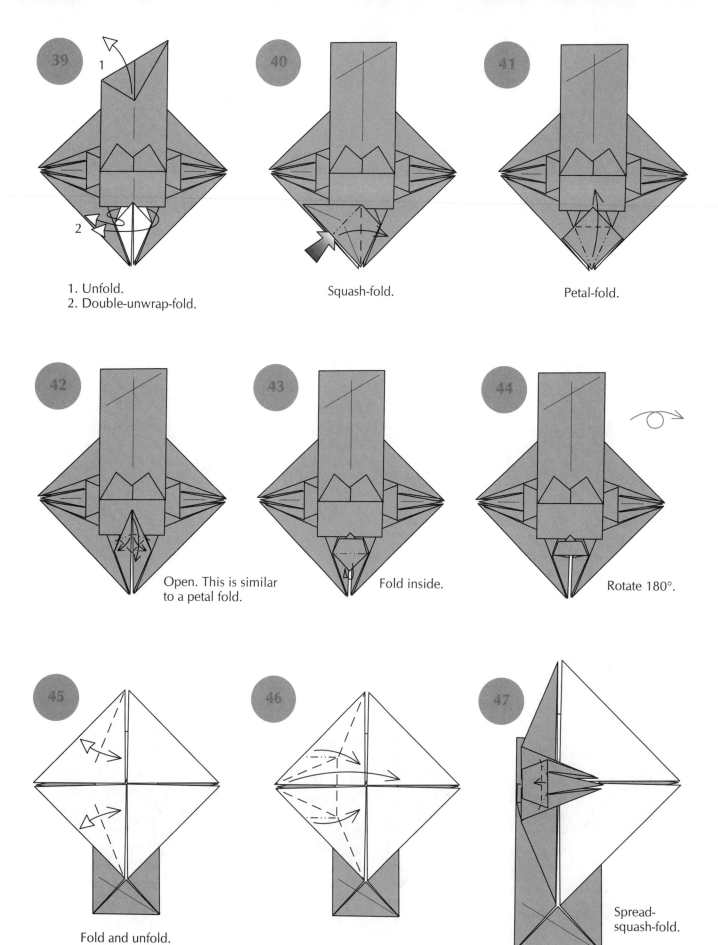

39

1. Unfold.
2. Double-unwrap-fold.

40

Squash-fold.

41

Petal-fold.

42

Open. This is similar
to a petal fold.

43

Fold inside.

44

Rotate 180°.

45

Fold and unfold.

46

47

Spread-
squash-fold.

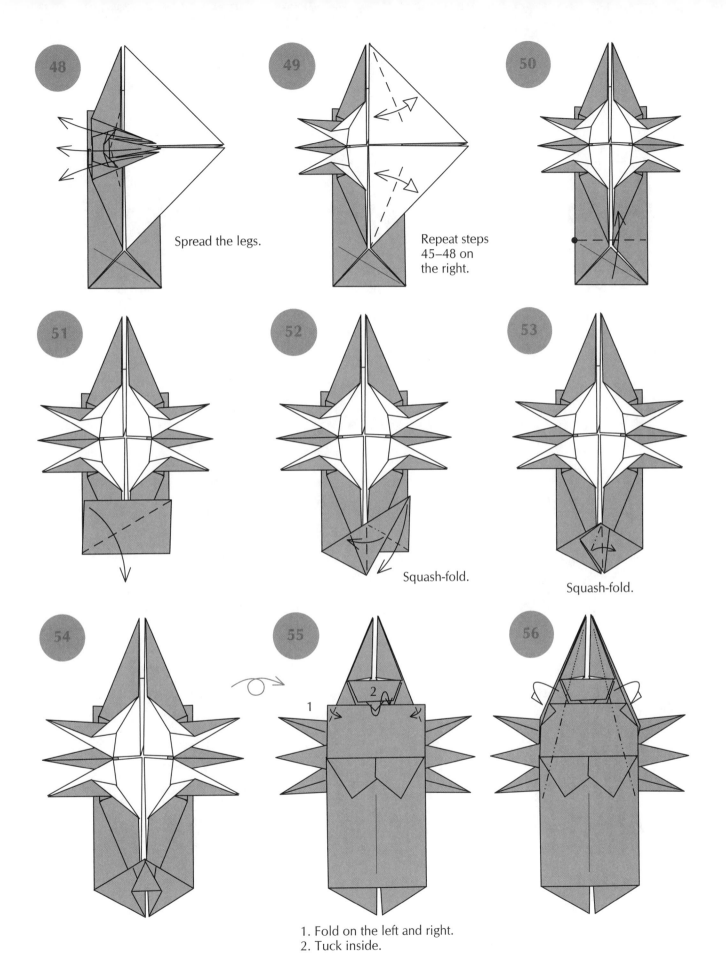

48 Spread the legs.

49 Repeat steps 45–48 on the right.

50

51

52 Squash-fold.

53 Squash-fold.

54

55

56

1. Fold on the left and right.
2. Tuck inside.

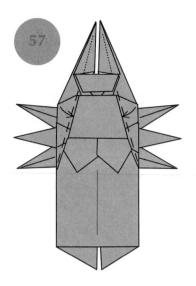

57

Tuck inside.

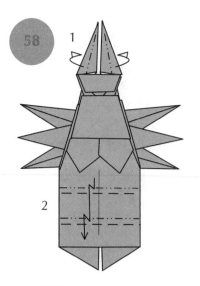

58

1

2

1. Fold both layers together at the antennae.
2. Pleat folds.

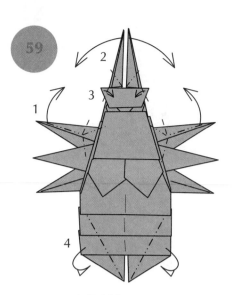

59

2

3

1

4

1. Rabbit ears.
2. Reverse folds.
3. Valley folds.
4. Mountain folds.

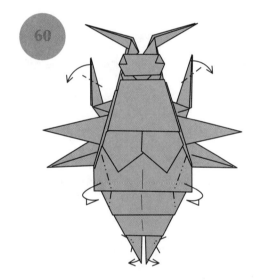

60

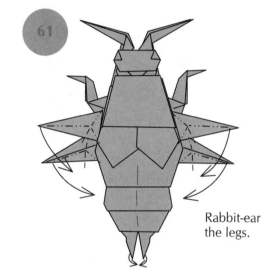

61

Rabbit-ear the legs.

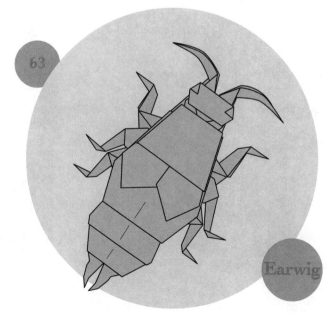

62

63

Earwig

Leaf Bug

The Leaf Bug has a very clever method of camouflage; it resembles the shape, size and color of a leaf, and it can stand still or wave lightly in the wind, fooling any would-be predator into passing right by.

1

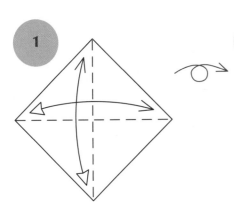

Fold and unfold.

2

Fold and unfold.

3

Fold to the center and unfold. Rotate.

4

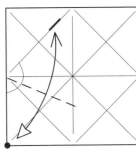

Fold and unfold.

5

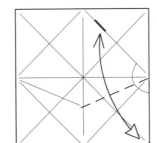

Fold and unfold.

6

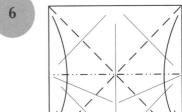

Make the waterbomb base.

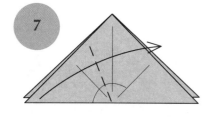

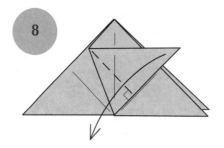

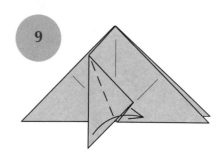

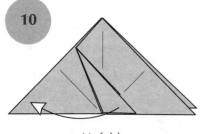

Unfold.

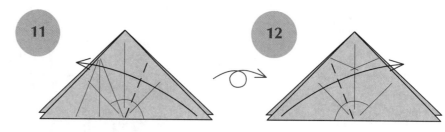

Repeat steps 7–10
on the right.

Repeat steps 7–11.

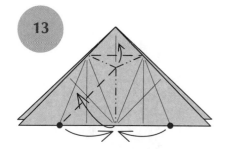

Lift up at the bottom.
The dots will meet.

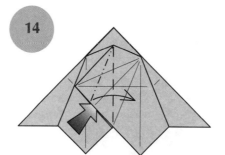

Squash-fold.

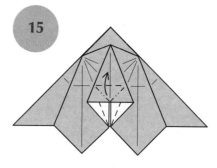

Petal-fold.

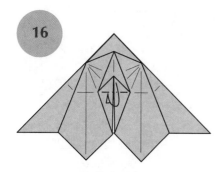

Tuck inside.

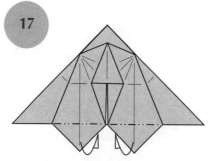

Tuck inside.

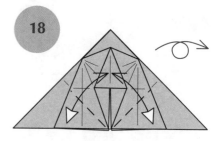

Fold and unfold.

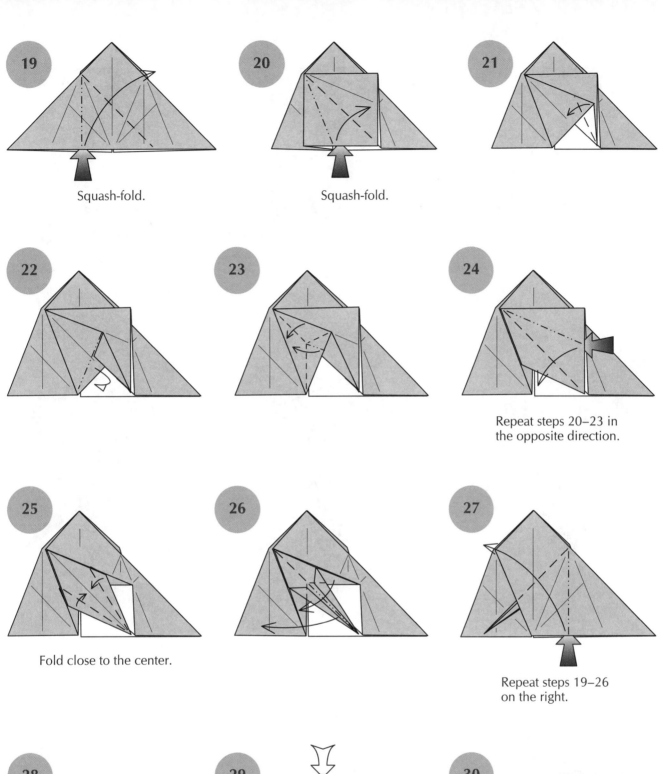

19 Squash-fold.

20 Squash-fold.

21

22

23

24 Repeat steps 20–23 in the opposite direction.

25 Fold close to the center.

26

27 Repeat steps 19–26 on the right.

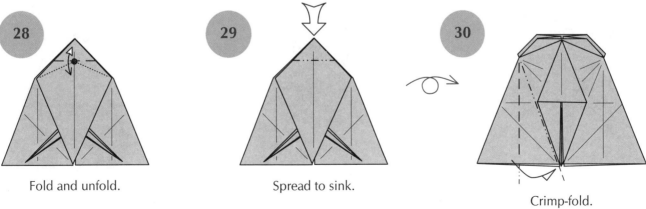

28 Fold and unfold.

29 Spread to sink.

30 Crimp-fold.

Leaf Bug 67

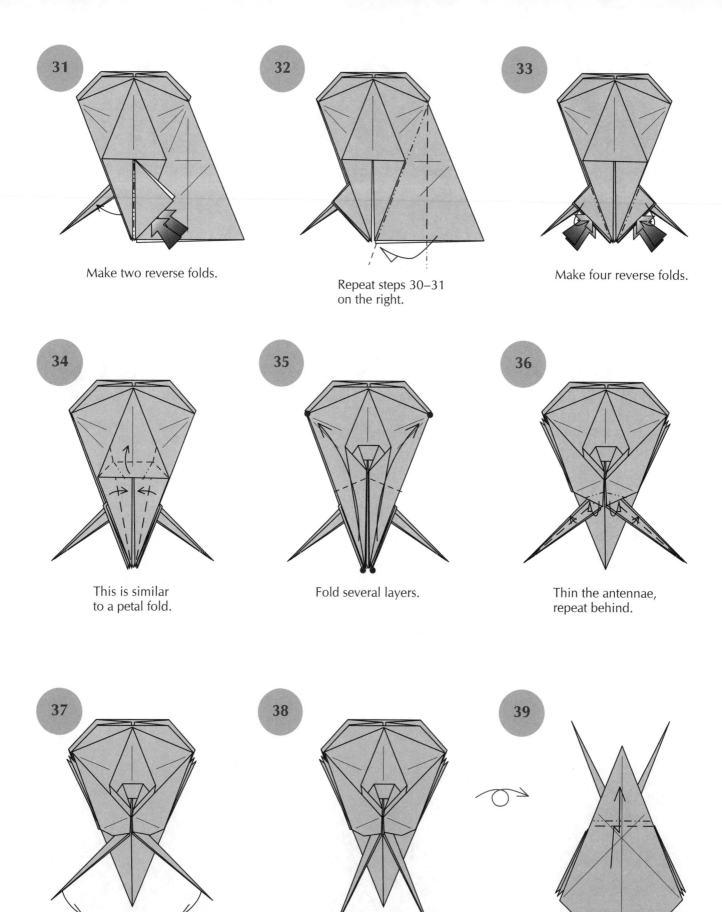

31 Make two reverse folds.

32 Repeat steps 30–31 on the right.

33 Make four reverse folds.

34 This is similar to a petal fold.

35 Fold several layers.

36 Thin the antennae, repeat behind.

37 Slide the antennae.

38 Rotate 180°.

39 Pleat-fold.

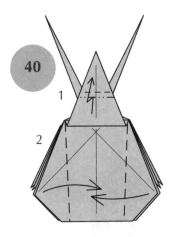

40

1. Pleat-fold.
2. Fold the top layers.

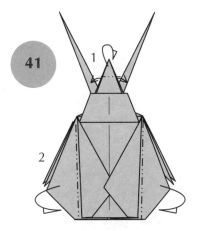

41

1. Fold behind and
   spread to form eyes.
2. Tuck inside.

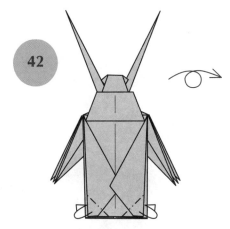

42

Repeat behind.

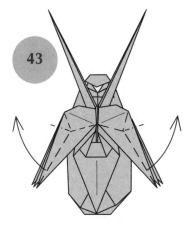

43

Rabbit ears. Fold the legs
on top and make small
spread-squash-folds.

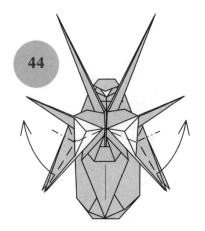

44

Repeat step 43
two times.

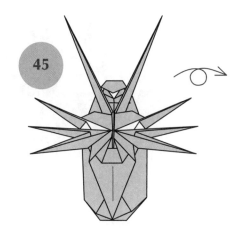

45

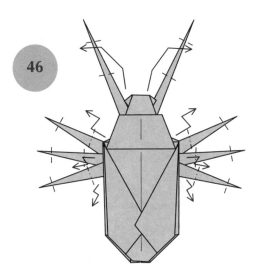

46

Shape the legs and antennae.

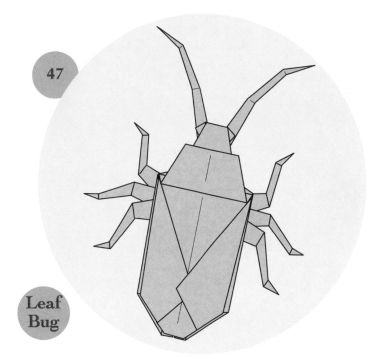

47

Leaf Bug

Leaf Bug 69

Cicada

The Cicada is a famous insect that can take many years to mature, all the while living underground. When the famous 17-Year Cicadas mature and seek mates, they can fill the air with their distinct song, and even preschoolers get excited by the arrival of these red-eyed singers.

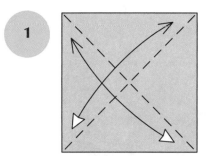

1

Fold and unfold.

2

Fold and unfold on the right.

3

Fold and unfold.

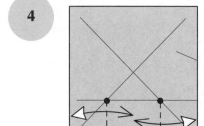

4

Fold and unfold.

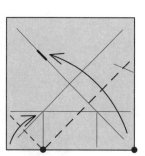

5

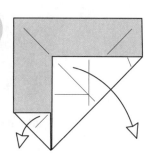

6

Unfold.

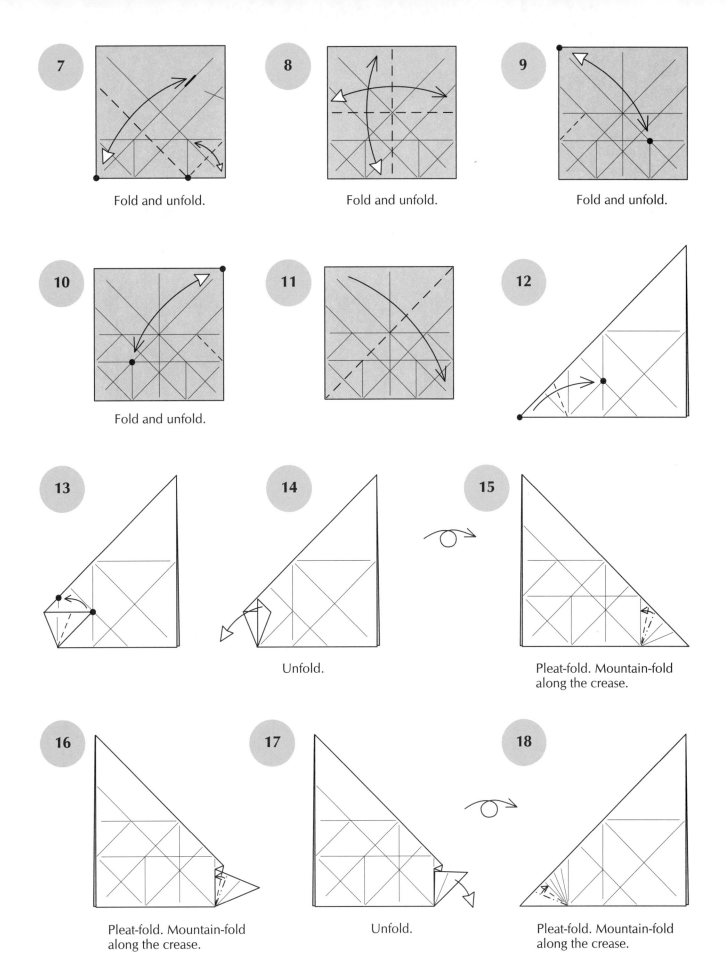

7 Fold and unfold.

8 Fold and unfold.

9 Fold and unfold.

10 Fold and unfold.

11

12

13

14 Unfold.

15 Pleat-fold. Mountain-fold along the crease.

16 Pleat-fold. Mountain-fold along the crease.

17 Unfold.

18 Pleat-fold. Mountain-fold along the crease.

Cicada 71

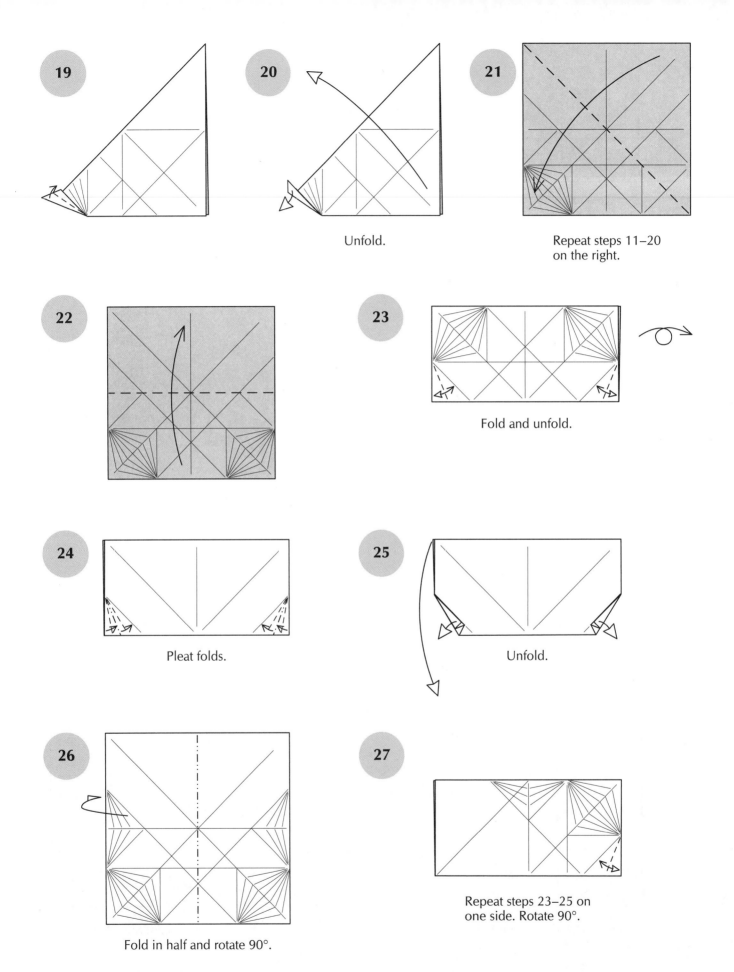

19

20

Unfold.

21

Repeat steps 11–20 on the right.

22

23

Fold and unfold.

24

Pleat folds.

25

Unfold.

26

Fold in half and rotate 90°.

27

Repeat steps 23–25 on one side. Rotate 90°.

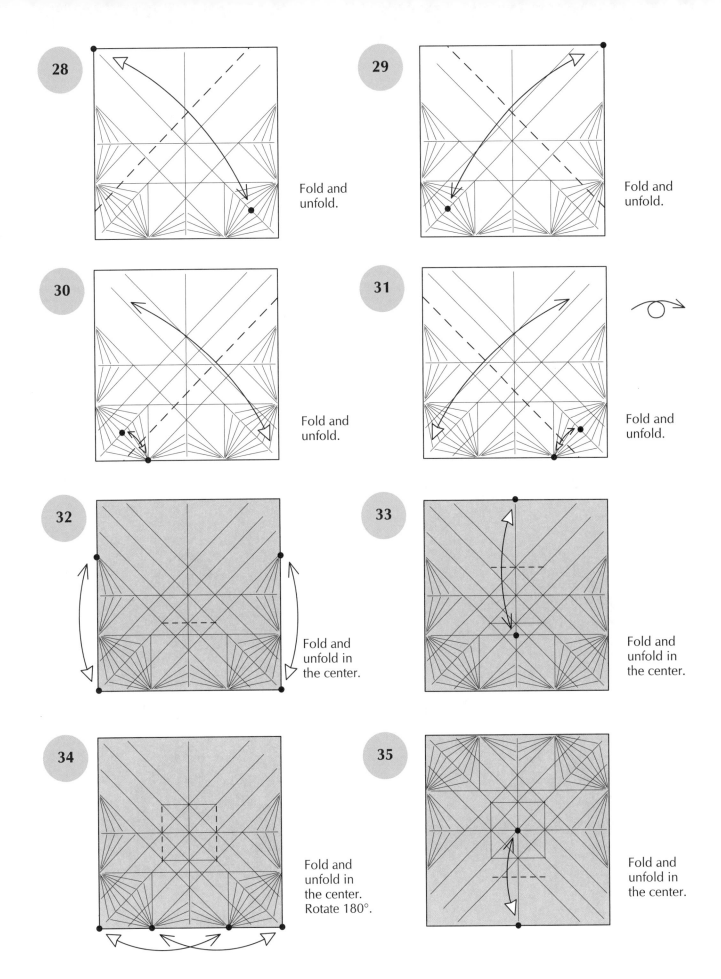

28 Fold and unfold.

29 Fold and unfold.

30 Fold and unfold.

31 Fold and unfold.

32 Fold and unfold in the center.

33 Fold and unfold in the center.

34 Fold and unfold in the center. Rotate 180°.

35 Fold and unfold in the center.

Cicada 73

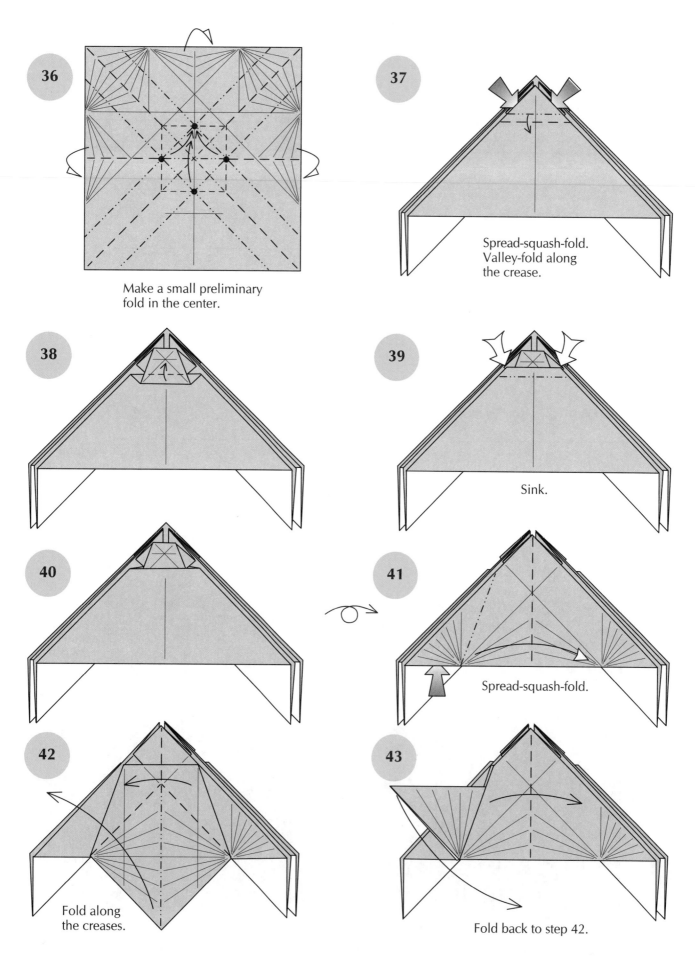

36 Make a small preliminary fold in the center.

37 Spread-squash-fold. Valley-fold along the crease.

38

39 Sink.

40

41 Spread-squash-fold.

42 Fold along the creases.

43 Fold back to step 42.

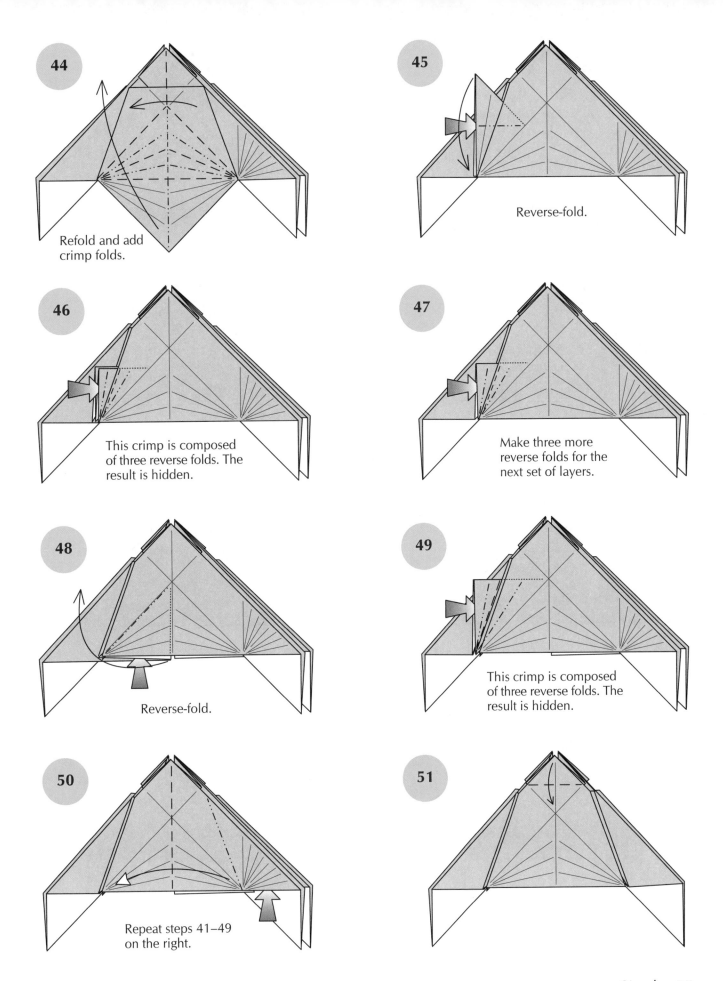

44 Refold and add crimp folds.

45 Reverse-fold.

46 This crimp is composed of three reverse folds. The result is hidden.

47 Make three more reverse folds for the next set of layers.

48 Reverse-fold.

49 This crimp is composed of three reverse folds. The result is hidden.

50 Repeat steps 41–49 on the right.

51

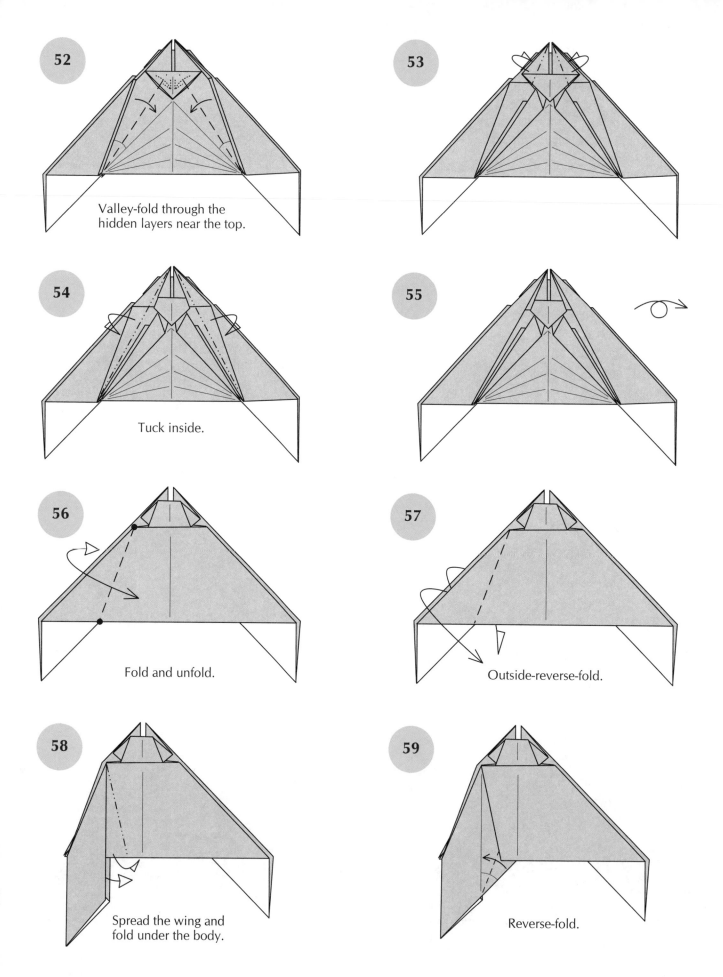

52 Valley-fold through the hidden layers near the top.

53

54 Tuck inside.

55

56 Fold and unfold.

57 Outside-reverse-fold.

58 Spread the wing and fold under the body.

59 Reverse-fold.

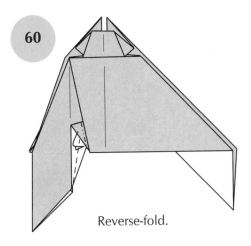

60

Reverse-fold.

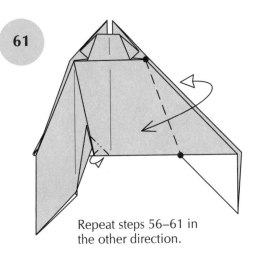

61

Repeat steps 56–61 in the other direction.

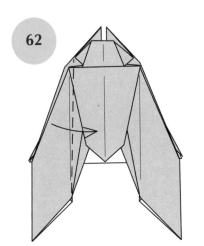

62

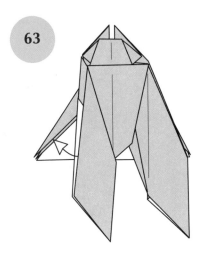

63

Pull out.

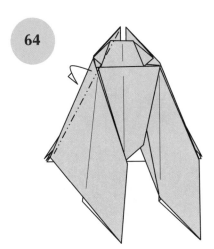

64

Tuck inside.

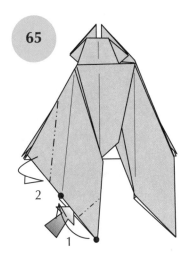

65

1. Reverse-fold.
2. Fold behind.

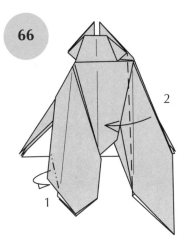

66

1. Fold behind
2. Repeat steps 62–66 in the other direction.

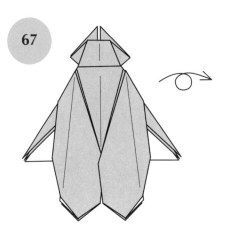

67

68

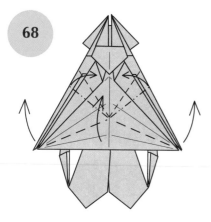

Fold the layers together.

69

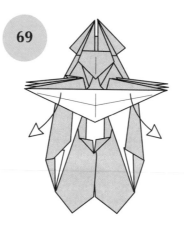

Unfold.

70

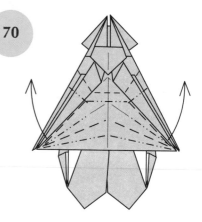

Pleat-fold the layers on the left and right, the layers will overlap in the center.

71

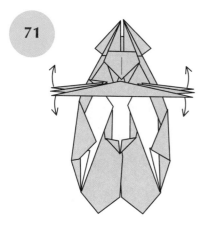

Separate the legs.

72

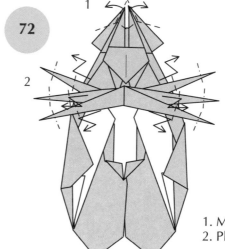

1. Make small rabbit ears.
2. Pleat-fold the legs.

73

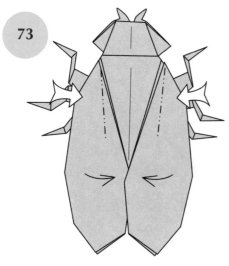

Shape the wings and body to make the cicada 3D.

74

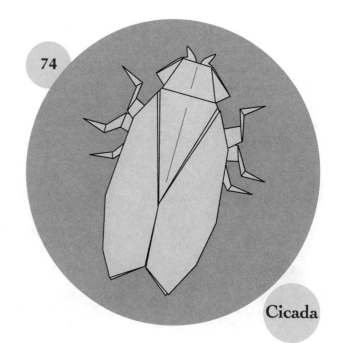

Cicada

Butterfly

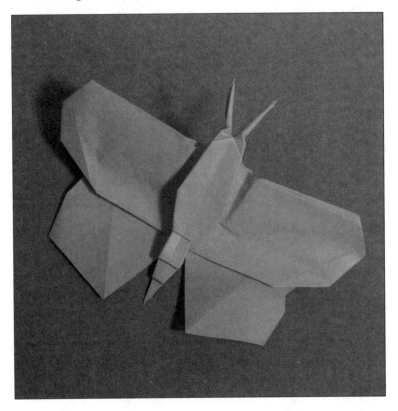

Butterflies are very colorful insects with four large wings. These wings are covered with tiny scales. Butterflies have a slender body and slender antennae. Many of the caterpillars we see are actually butterflies in their larval stage.

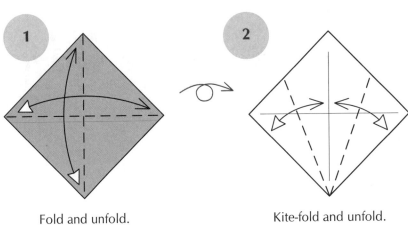

1 Fold and unfold.

2 Kite-fold and unfold.

3

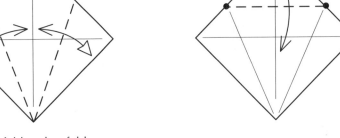

4 Fold and unfold.

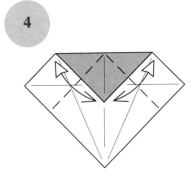

5

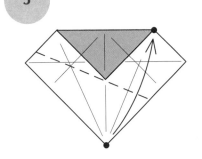

6 Squash-fold.

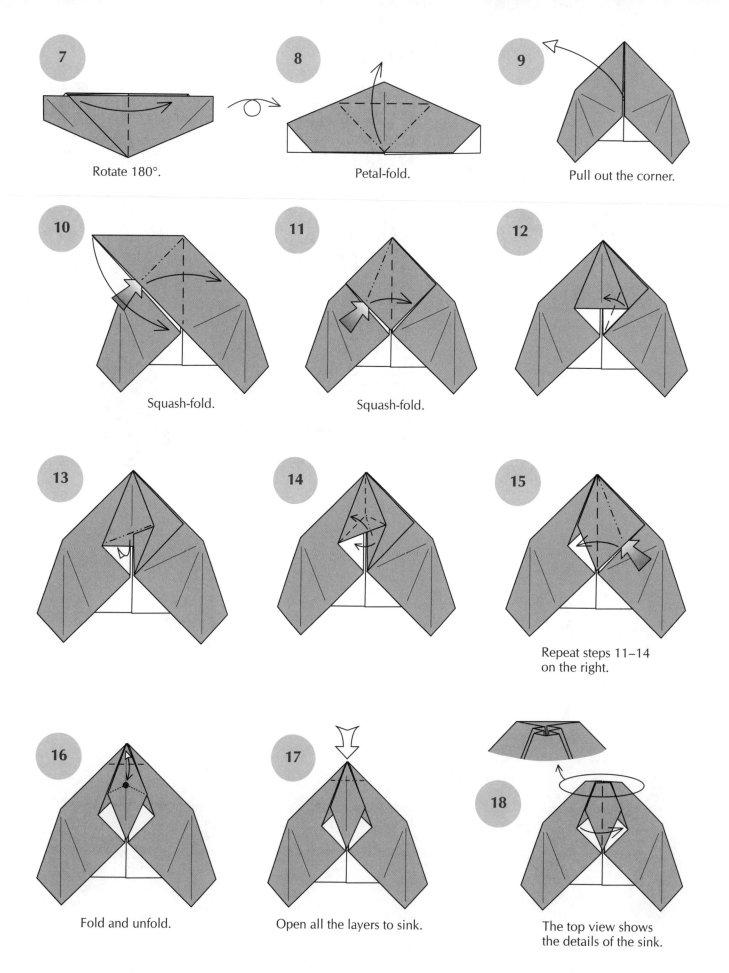

7

Rotate 180°.

8

Petal-fold.

9

Pull out the corner.

10

Squash-fold.

11

Squash-fold.

12

13

14

15

Repeat steps 11–14 on the right.

16

Fold and unfold.

17

Open all the layers to sink.

18

The top view shows the details of the sink.

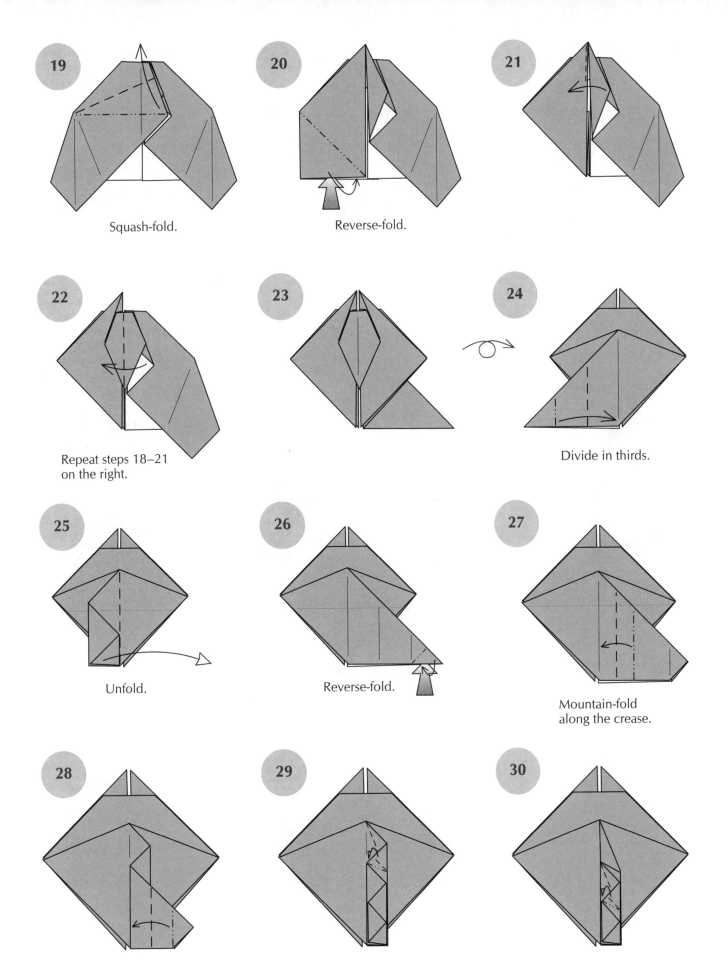

19 Squash-fold.

20 Reverse-fold.

21

22 Repeat steps 18–21 on the right.

23

24 Divide in thirds.

25 Unfold.

26 Reverse-fold.

27 Mountain-fold along the crease.

28

29

30

Butterfly 81

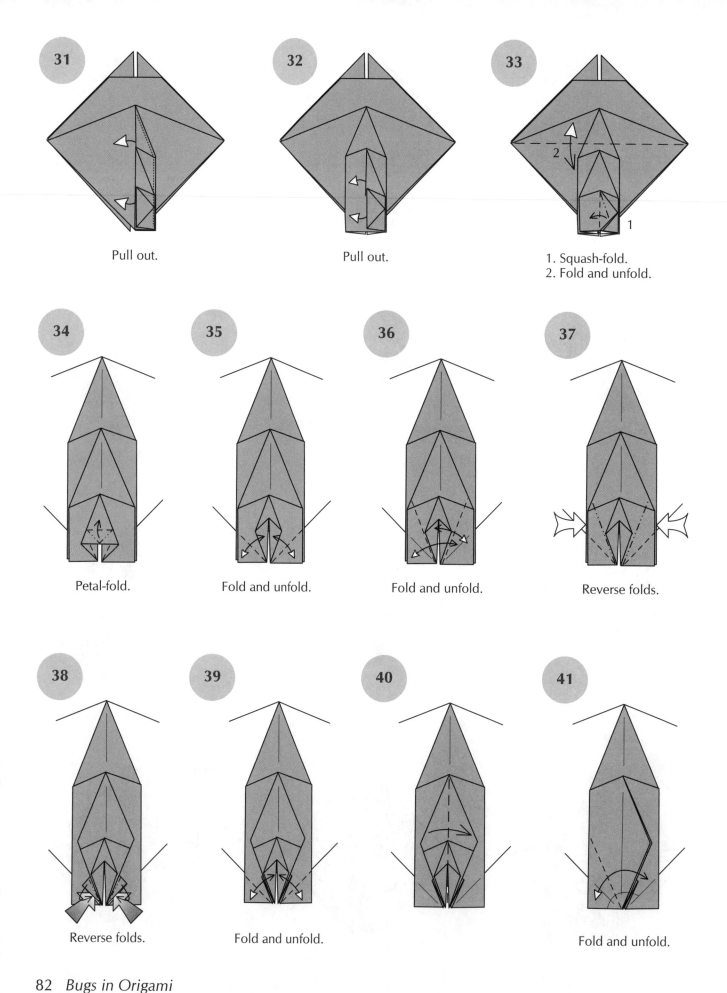

31

Pull out.

32

Pull out.

33

1. Squash-fold.
2. Fold and unfold.

34

Petal-fold.

35

Fold and unfold.

36

Fold and unfold.

37

Reverse folds.

38

Reverse folds.

39

Fold and unfold.

40

41

Fold and unfold.

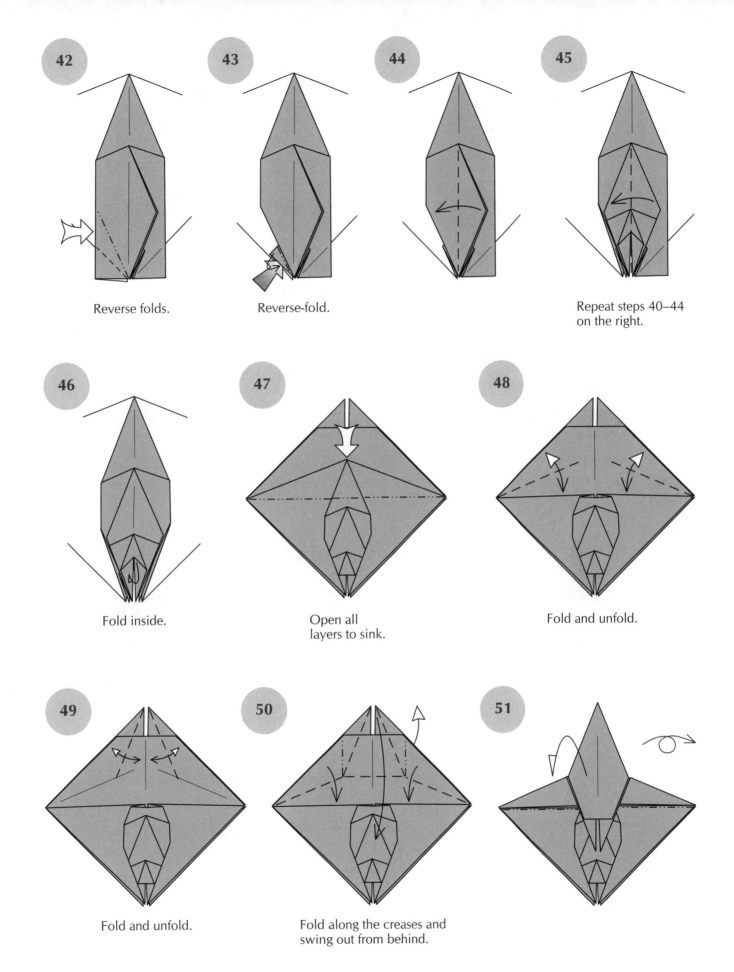

42 Reverse folds.

43 Reverse-fold.

44

45 Repeat steps 40–44 on the right.

46 Fold inside.

47 Open all layers to sink.

48 Fold and unfold.

49 Fold and unfold.

50 Fold along the creases and swing out from behind.

51

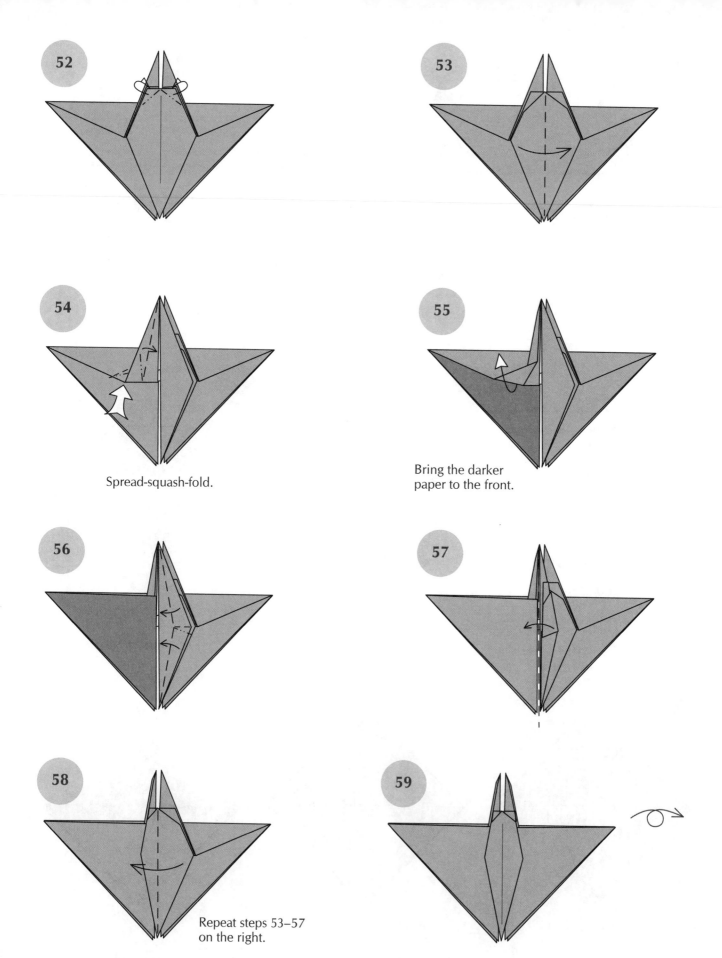

52

53

54

Spread-squash-fold.

55

Bring the darker
paper to the front.

56

57

58

Repeat steps 53–57
on the right.

59

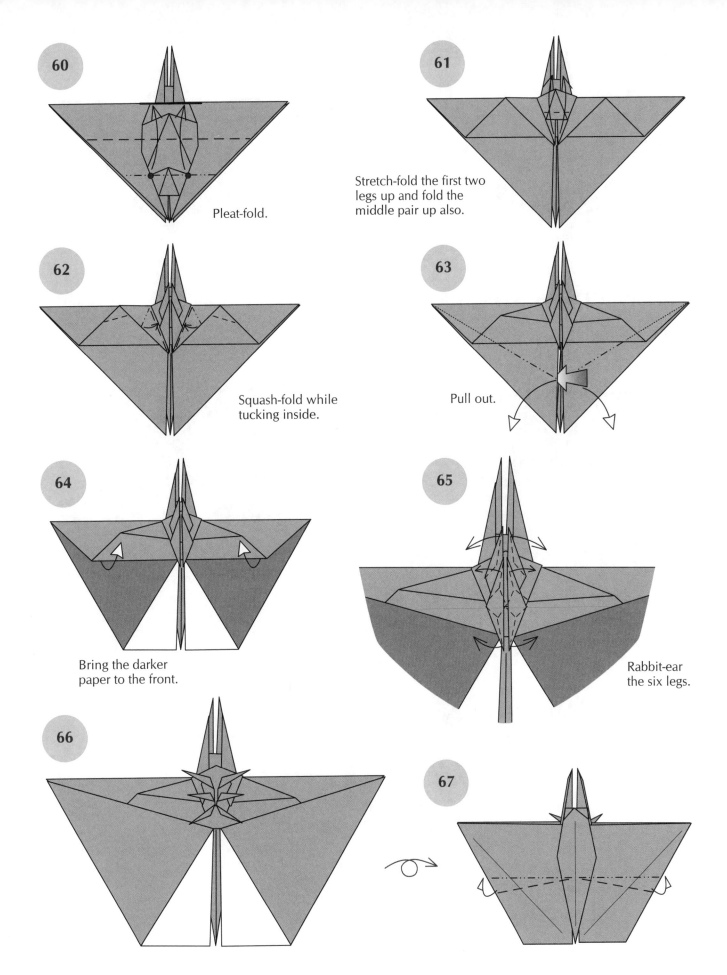

60 Pleat-fold.

61 Stretch-fold the first two legs up and fold the middle pair up also.

62 Squash-fold while tucking inside.

63 Pull out.

64 Bring the darker paper to the front.

65 Rabbit-ear the six legs.

66

67

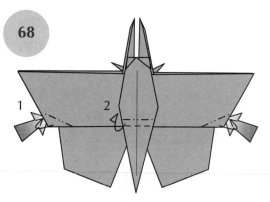

68

1. Reverse-fold the wings.
2. Pleat-fold.

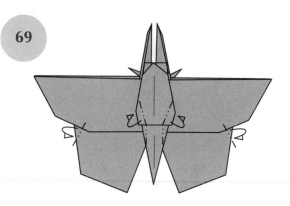

69

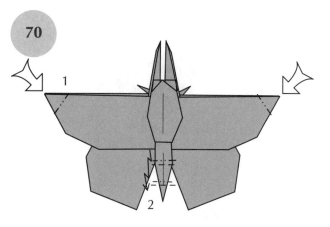

70

1. Sink the wing tips.
2. Pleat-fold the tail.

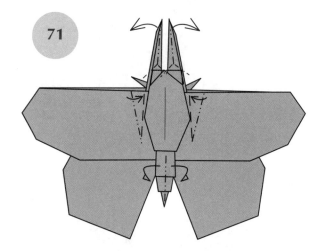

71

Thin the antennae. Bend the
tail. Lift the wings up slightly.

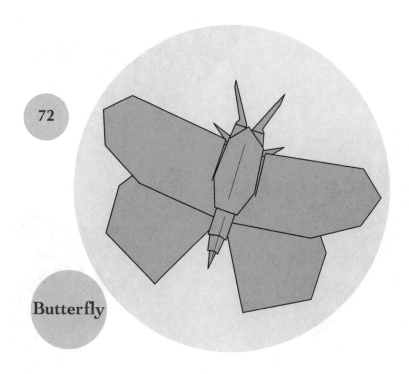

72

Butterfly

Scavenger Beetle

The Scavenger Beetle is a large beetle that can be found feeding on dead plants at the edge of ponds. The Scavenger Beetle has a distinctive ridge on its back. In order to breathe, it keeps an air bubble trapped underneath its body while it is in the water.

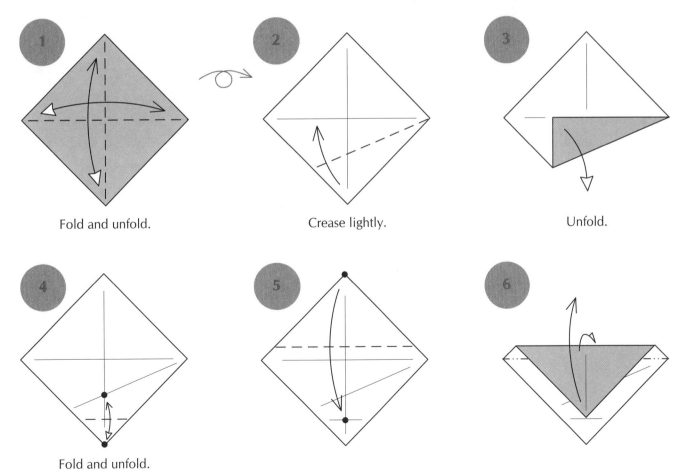

1. Fold and unfold.

2. Crease lightly.

3. Unfold.

4. Fold and unfold.

5.

6.

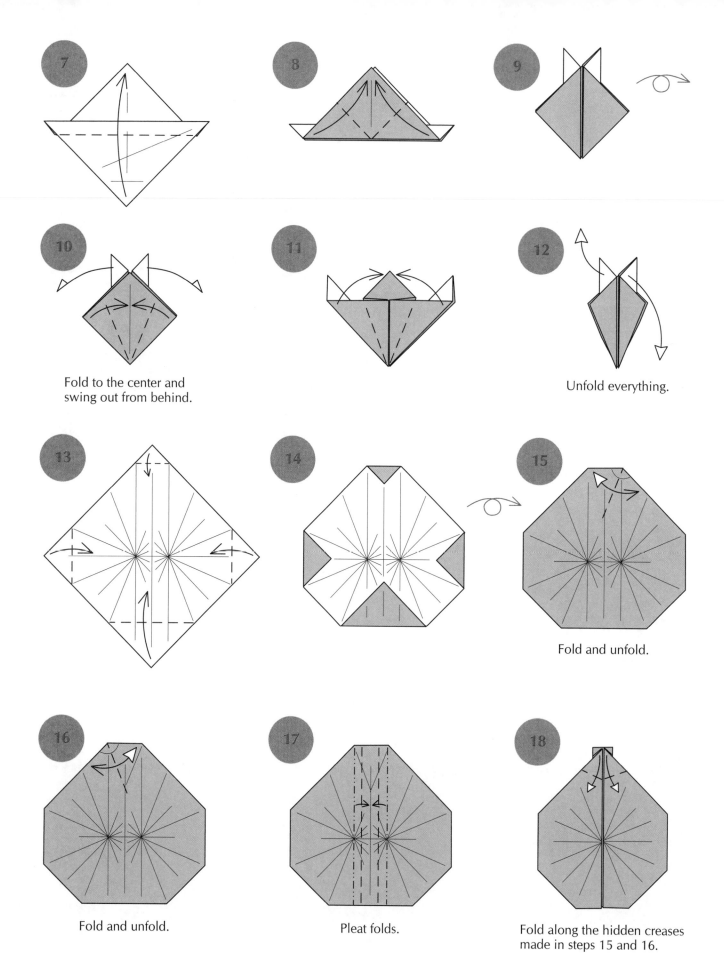

10 Fold to the center and swing out from behind.

12 Unfold everything.

15 Fold and unfold.

16 Fold and unfold.

17 Pleat folds.

18 Fold along the hidden creases made in steps 15 and 16.

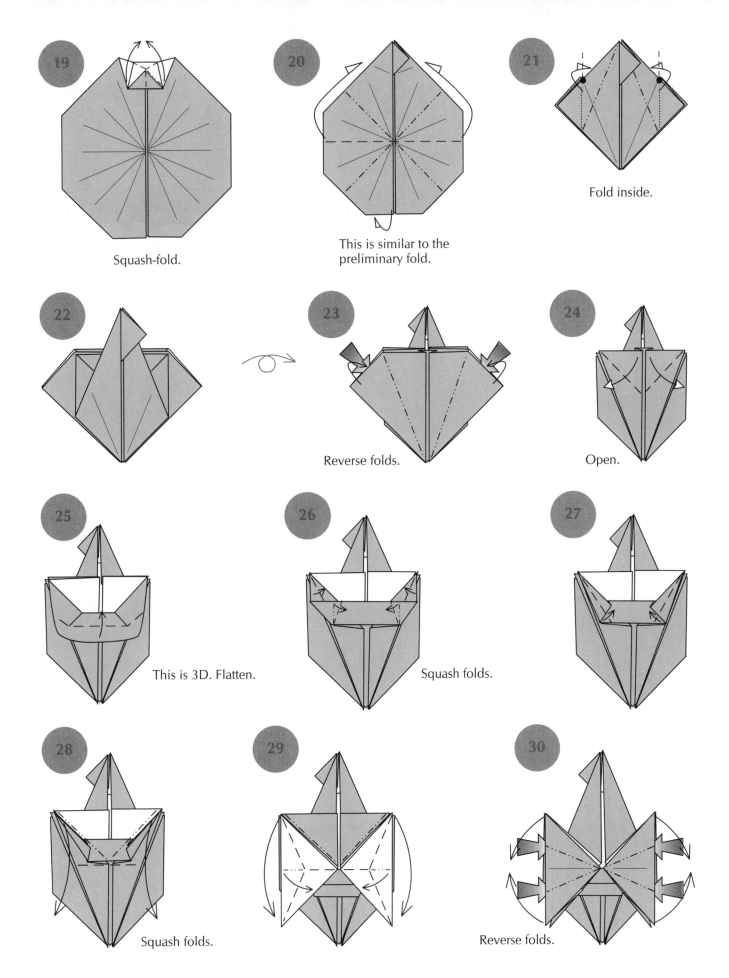

19 Squash-fold.

20 This is similar to the preliminary fold.

21 Fold inside.

22

23 Reverse folds.

24 Open.

25 This is 3D. Flatten.

26 Squash folds.

27

28 Squash folds.

29

30 Reverse folds.

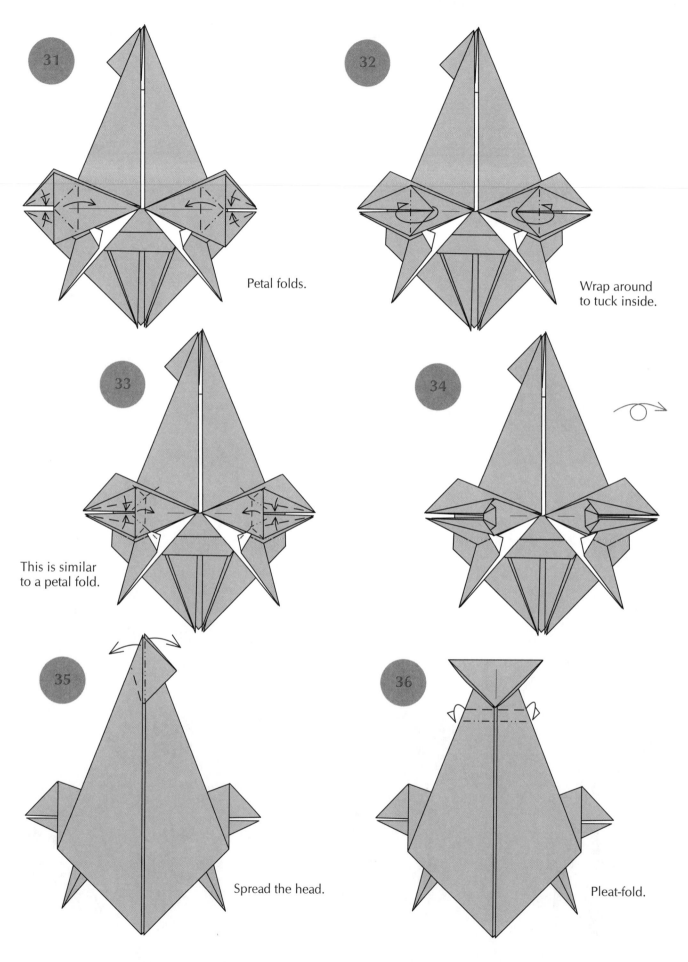

31 Petal folds.

32 Wrap around to tuck inside.

33 This is similar to a petal fold.

34

35 Spread the head.

36 Pleat-fold.

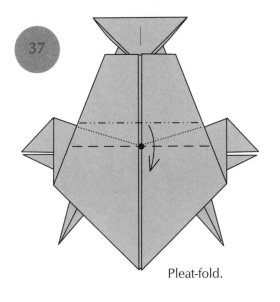

37

Pleat-fold.

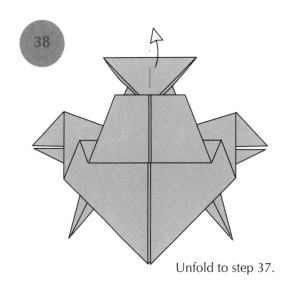

38

Unfold to step 37.

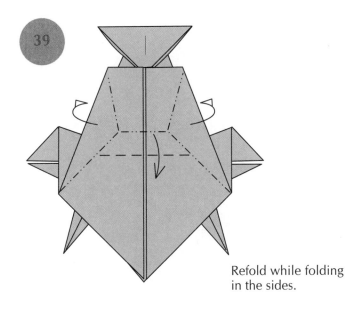

39

Refold while folding
in the sides.

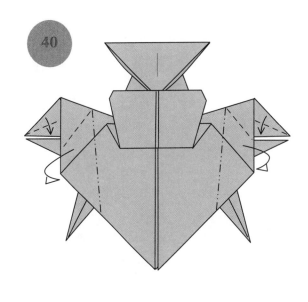

40

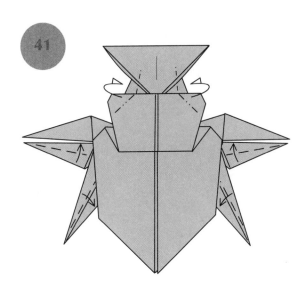

41

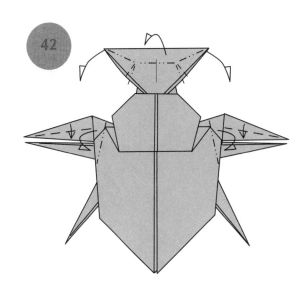

42

Scavenger Beetle 91

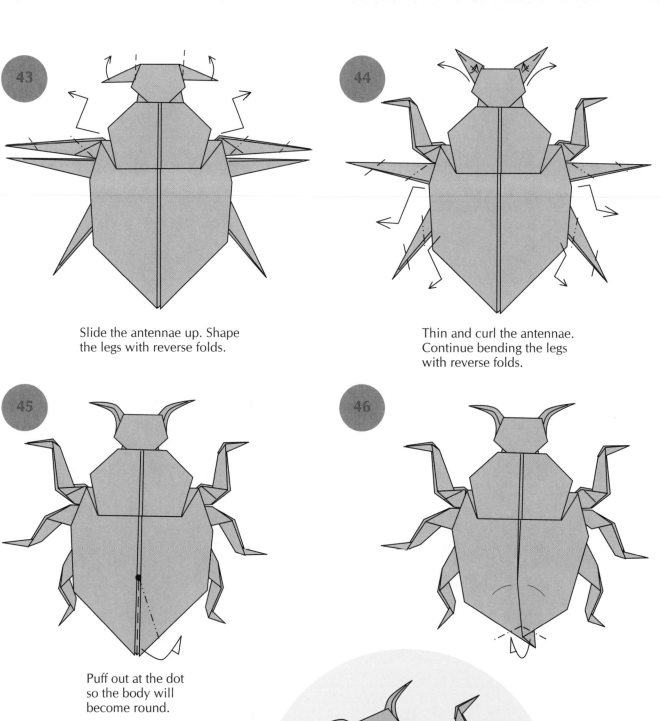

43 Slide the antennae up. Shape the legs with reverse folds.

44 Thin and curl the antennae. Continue bending the legs with reverse folds.

45 Puff out at the dot so the body will become round.

46

47 Scavenger Beetle

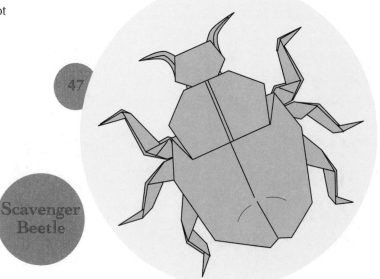

Ladybug

Ladybugs are small, brightly colored beetles. Generally under 1/4 inch long, they are oval in shape, have short legs, and are red or yellow with black spots or black with red or yellow spots. Ladybugs feed on destructive, plant-eating insects; adults are frequently used in pest control.

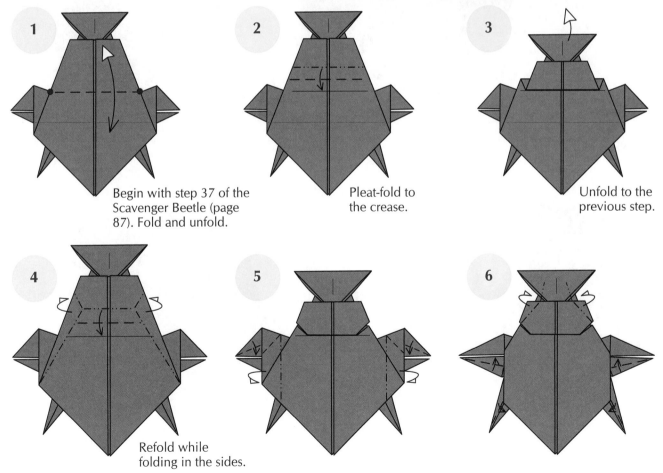

1 — Begin with step 37 of the Scavenger Beetle (page 87). Fold and unfold.

2 — Pleat-fold to the crease.

3 — Unfold to the previous step.

4 — Refold while folding in the sides.

5

6

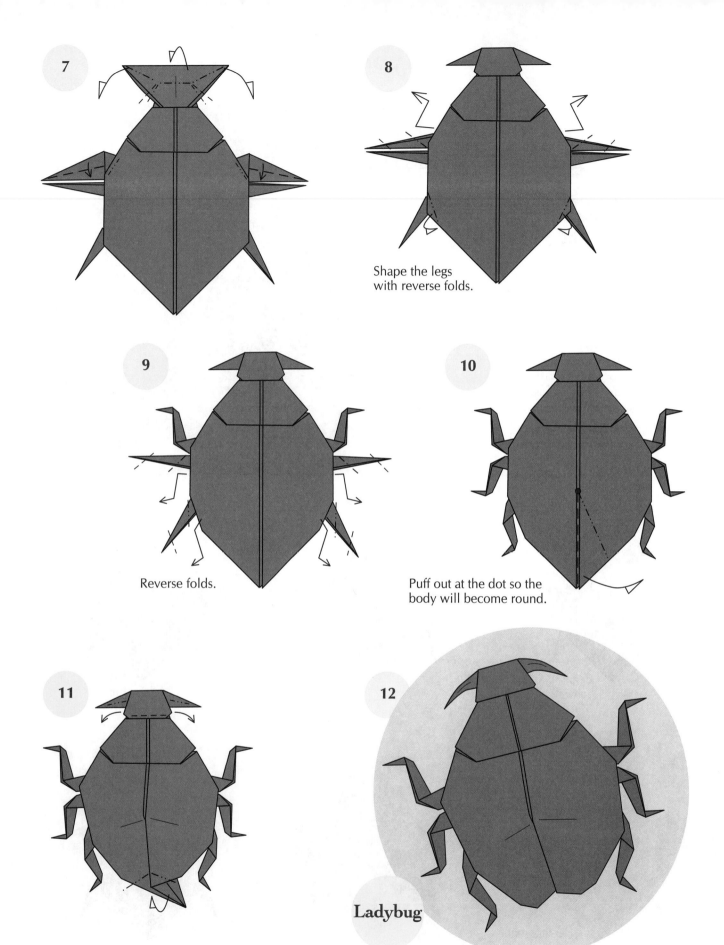

7

8

Shape the legs
with reverse folds.

9

Reverse folds.

10

Puff out at the dot so the
body will become round.

11

12

Ladybug

Long-Horned Beetle

The Long-horned Beetle is one of the most destructive plant pests in the world. At 1 1/4 inches long, this insect is coal black with irregular white spots on its back. The females chew notches in the bark of trees and deposit their eggs there. After the beetles mature, they burrow out of the tree in late Spring or Summer leaving small holes in the trees. Adult beetles feed on the leaves and bark of trees.

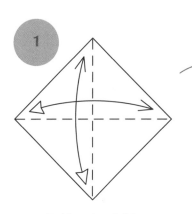

Fold and unfold.

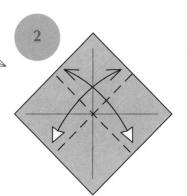

Fold and unfold.

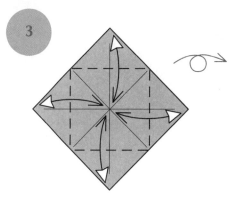

Fold to the center and unfold. Rotate.

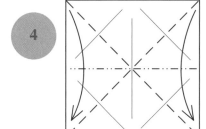

Make the waterbomb base.

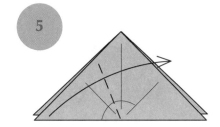

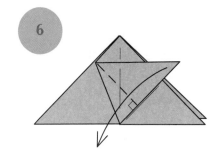

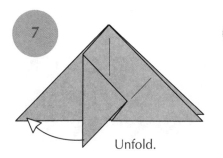

7 Unfold.

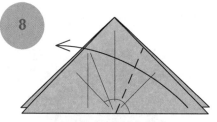

8 Repeat steps 5–7 on the right.

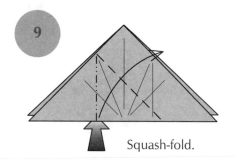

9 Squash-fold.

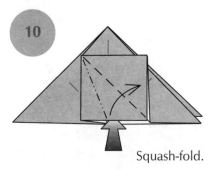

10 Squash-fold.

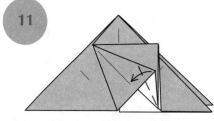

11

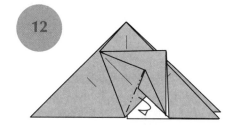

12

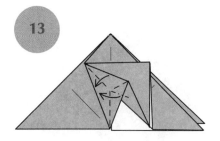

13

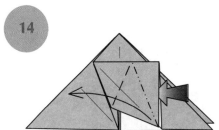

14 Squash-fold.

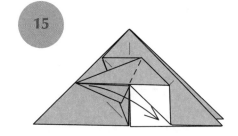

15

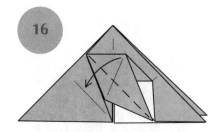

16

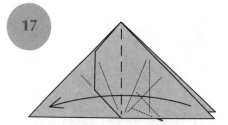

17 Fold the outer layer to the left while keeping the inner flap at the right.

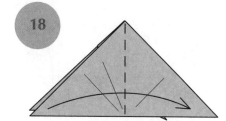

18

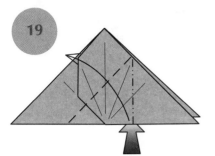

Repeat steps 9–16
on the right.

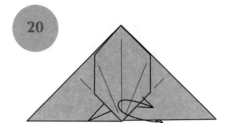

Pull out the flap.

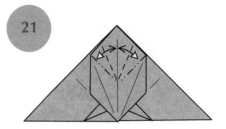

Fold and unfold the top layers.

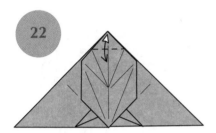

Fold and unfold.

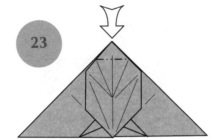

Spread to sink.

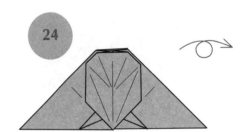

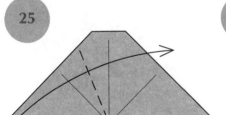

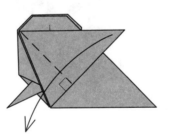

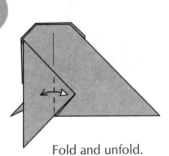

Fold and unfold.

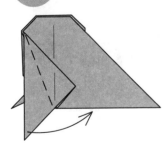

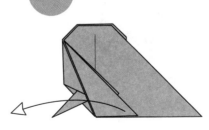

Unfold.

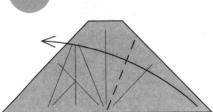

Repeat steps 25–29
on the right.

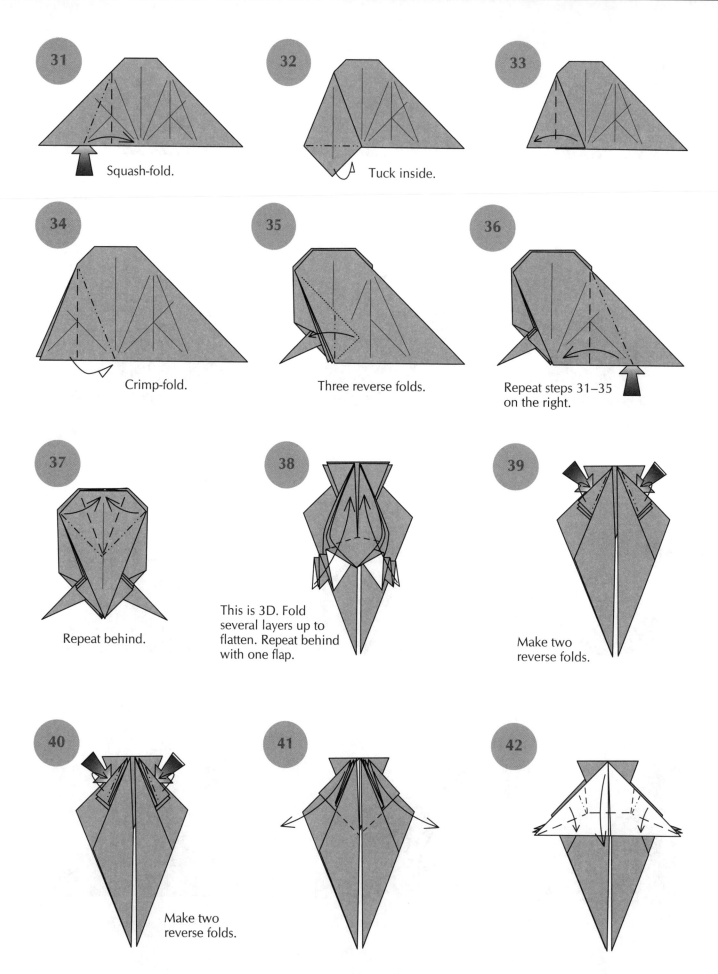

31 Squash-fold.

32 Tuck inside.

33

34 Crimp-fold.

35 Three reverse folds.

36 Repeat steps 31–35 on the right.

37 Repeat behind.

38 This is 3D. Fold several layers up to flatten. Repeat behind with one flap.

39 Make two reverse folds.

40 Make two reverse folds.

41

42

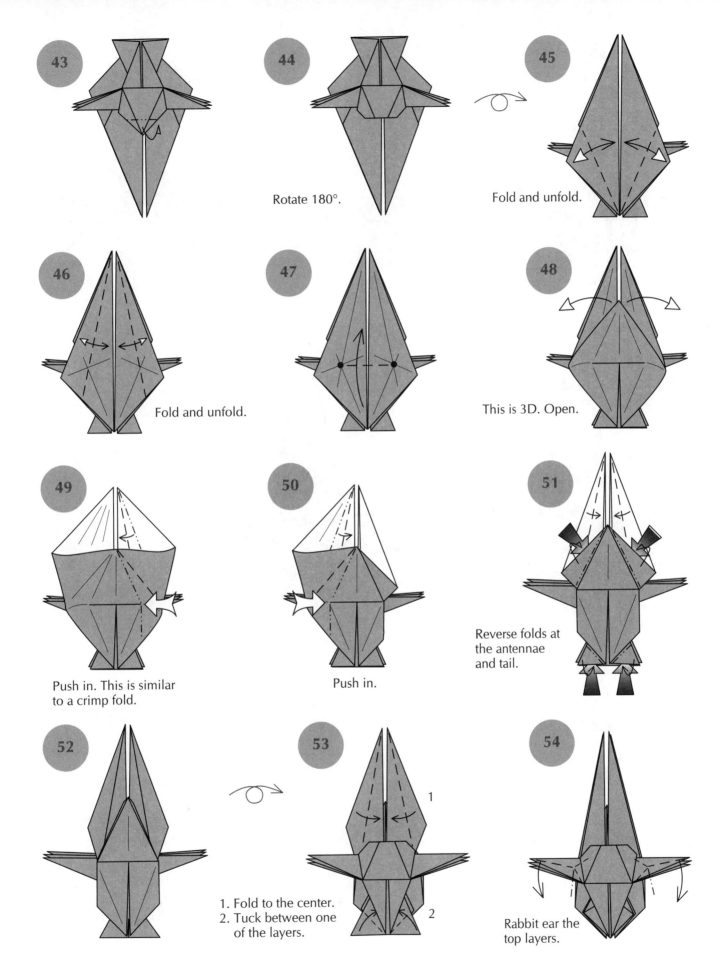

43

44

Rotate 180°.

45

Fold and unfold.

46

Fold and unfold.

47

48

This is 3D. Open.

49

Push in. This is similar to a crimp fold.

50

Push in.

51

Reverse folds at the antennae and tail.

52

53

1. Fold to the center.
2. Tuck between one of the layers.

54

Rabbit ear the top layers.

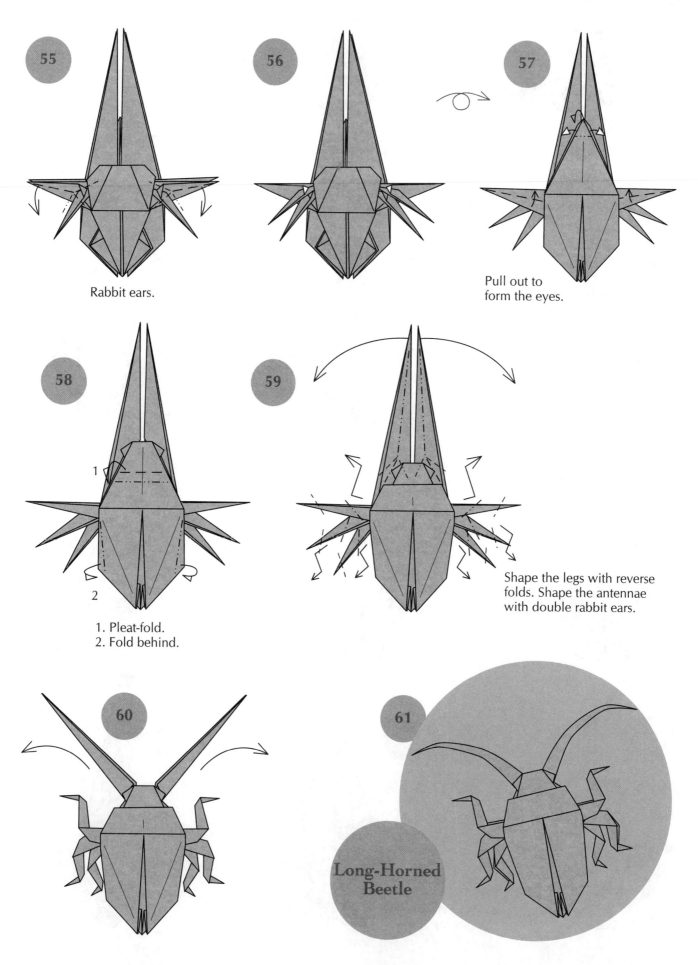

55

Rabbit ears.

56

57

Pull out to form the eyes.

58

1
2

1. Pleat-fold.
2. Fold behind.

59

Shape the legs with reverse folds. Shape the antennae with double rabbit ears.

60

61

Long-Horned Beetle

Tiger Beetle

The Tiger Beetle is an aggressive member of the Beetle family, and some species can run very fast. Their coloring resembles the pattern of a tiger's coat, and like their namesakes, they can be fierce predators.

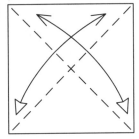

Fold and unfold.

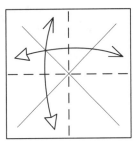

Fold and unfold.

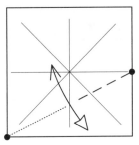

Fold and unfold.

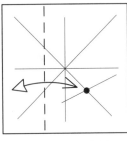

Fold and unfold
to the dot.

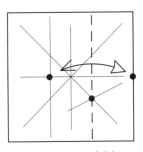

Fold and unfold.

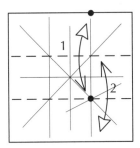

Fold and unfold.
Rotate.

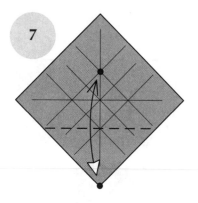

7

Fold and unfold.
Rotate 90°.

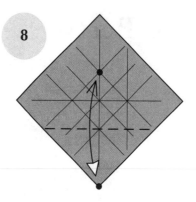

8

Repeat step 7 three times.

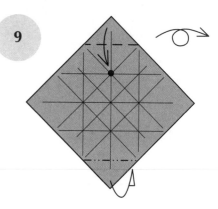

9

Rotate.

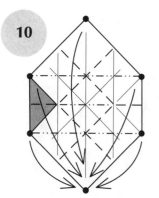

10

Fold along the creases.
The dots will meet.

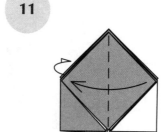

11

Repeat behind.

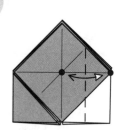

12

Fold and unfold.

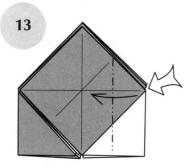

13

Spread-squash-fold.

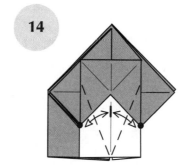

14

Fold and unfold.

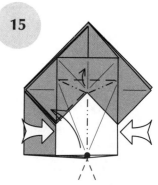

15

Lift up at the bottom dot. This
is similar to a spread squash
fold and a squash fold.

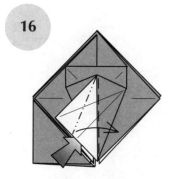

16

Squash-fold.

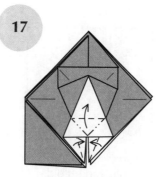

17

Petal-fold.

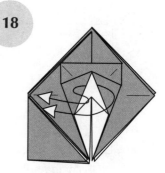

18

Double-unwrap-fold.

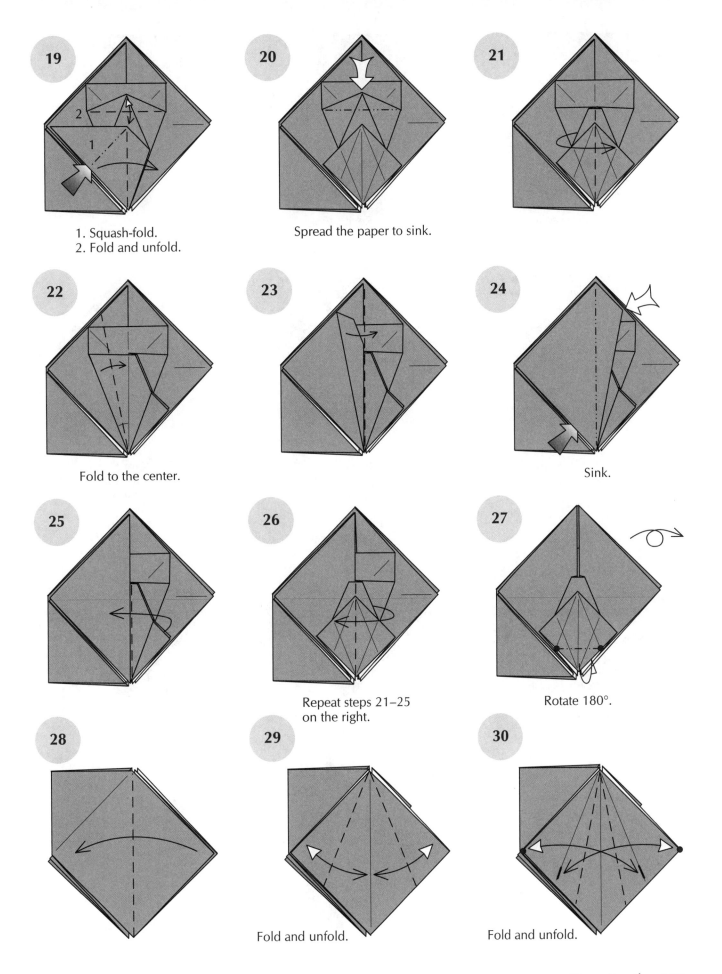

19

1. Squash-fold.
2. Fold and unfold.

20

Spread the paper to sink.

21

22

Fold to the center.

23

24

Sink.

25

26

Repeat steps 21–25
on the right.

27

Rotate 180°.

28

29

Fold and unfold.

30

Fold and unfold.

Tiger Beetle 103

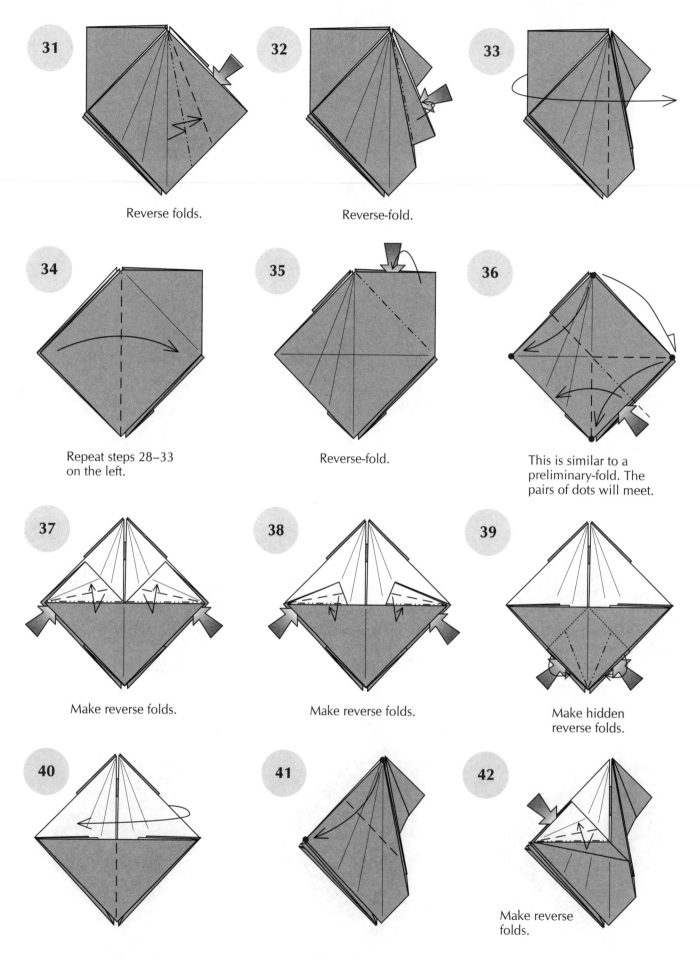

31

Reverse folds.

32

Reverse-fold.

33

34

Repeat steps 28–33
on the left.

35

Reverse-fold.

36

This is similar to a
preliminary-fold. The
pairs of dots will meet.

37

Make reverse folds.

38

Make reverse folds.

39

Make hidden
reverse folds.

40

41

42

Make reverse
folds.

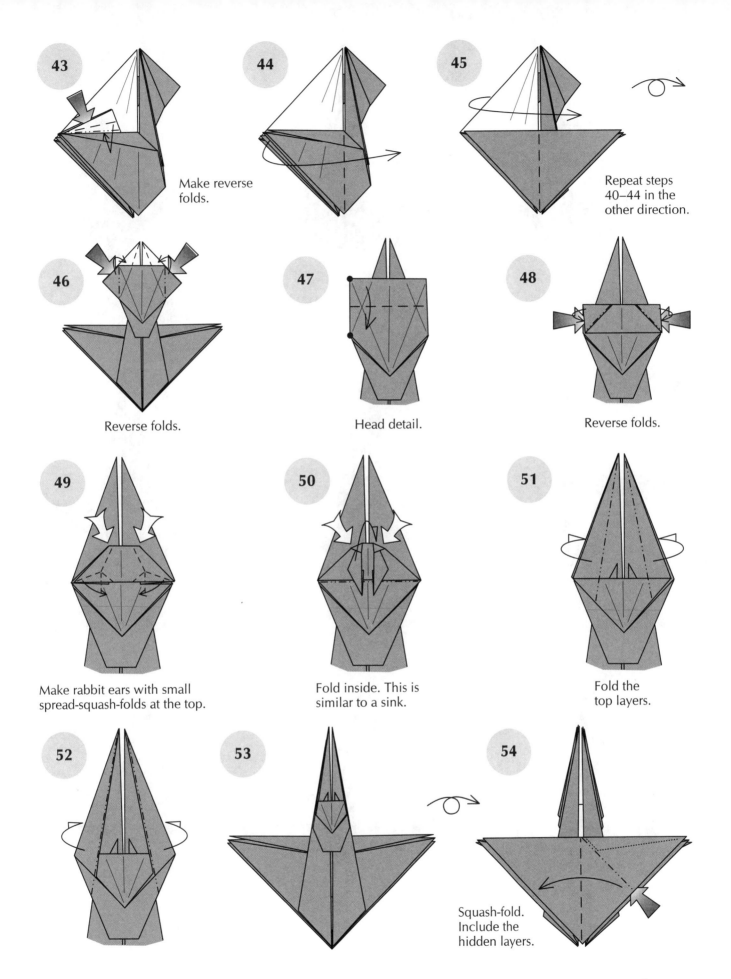

43 Make reverse folds.

44

45 Repeat steps 40–44 in the other direction.

46 Reverse folds.

47 Head detail.

48 Reverse folds.

49 Make rabbit ears with small spread-squash-folds at the top.

50 Fold inside. This is similar to a sink.

51 Fold the top layers.

52

53

54 Squash-fold. Include the hidden layers.

Tiger Beetle 105

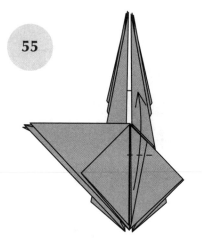

55

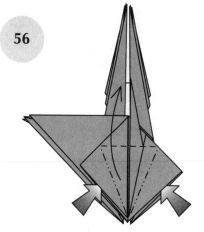

56

Petal-fold.

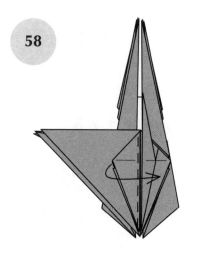

57

Fold the top layers to the edges while folding down.

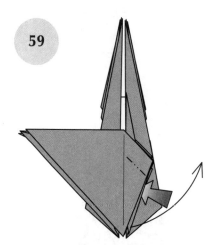

58

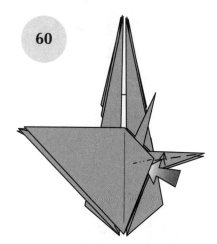

59

Reverse-fold two legs together.

60

Thin the leg with a small reverse fold by the base. Repeat behind.

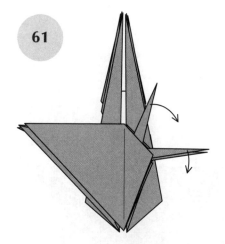

61

Pivot two legs.

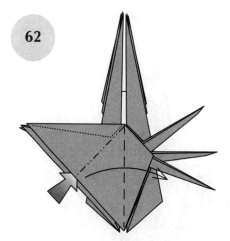

62

Repeat steps 54–61 on the left.

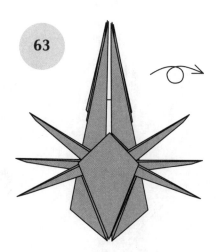

63

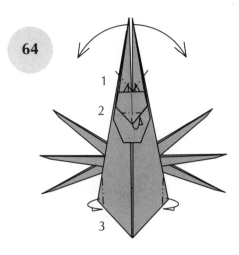

64

1. Reverse folds.
2. Fold behind.
3. Fold behind.

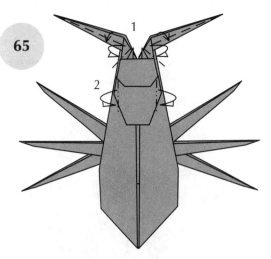

65

1. Thin the antennae with small reverse folds by the base. Repeat behind.
2. Fold behind.

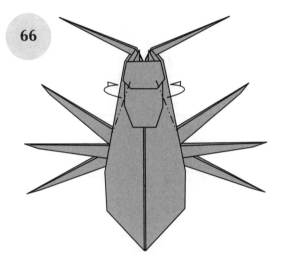

66

Fold behind.

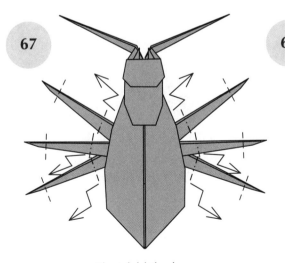

67

Pleat-fold the legs.

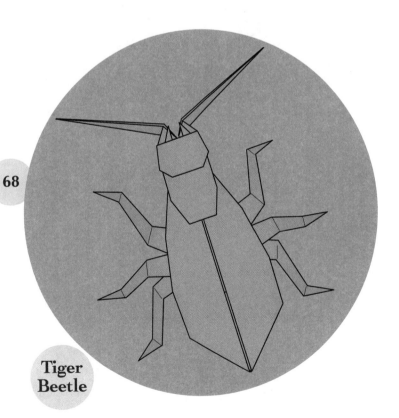

68

Tiger Beetle

Weevil

The Weevil is a member of the snout beetle family. It has a hard body and a long head pointing downward. This insect is a pest which does much damage to grain, cotton, nut, and other crops. It is about 1/16 to 1/2 an inch long. Most are gray, black, or brown, but some are bright blue and green.

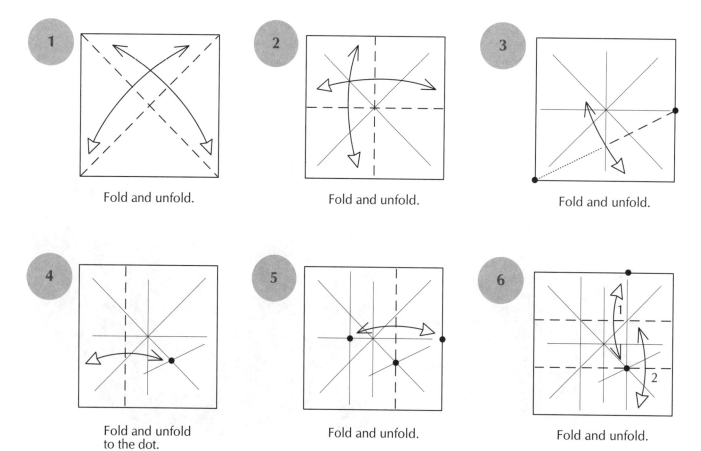

1 Fold and unfold.

2 Fold and unfold.

3 Fold and unfold.

4 Fold and unfold to the dot.

5 Fold and unfold.

6 Fold and unfold.

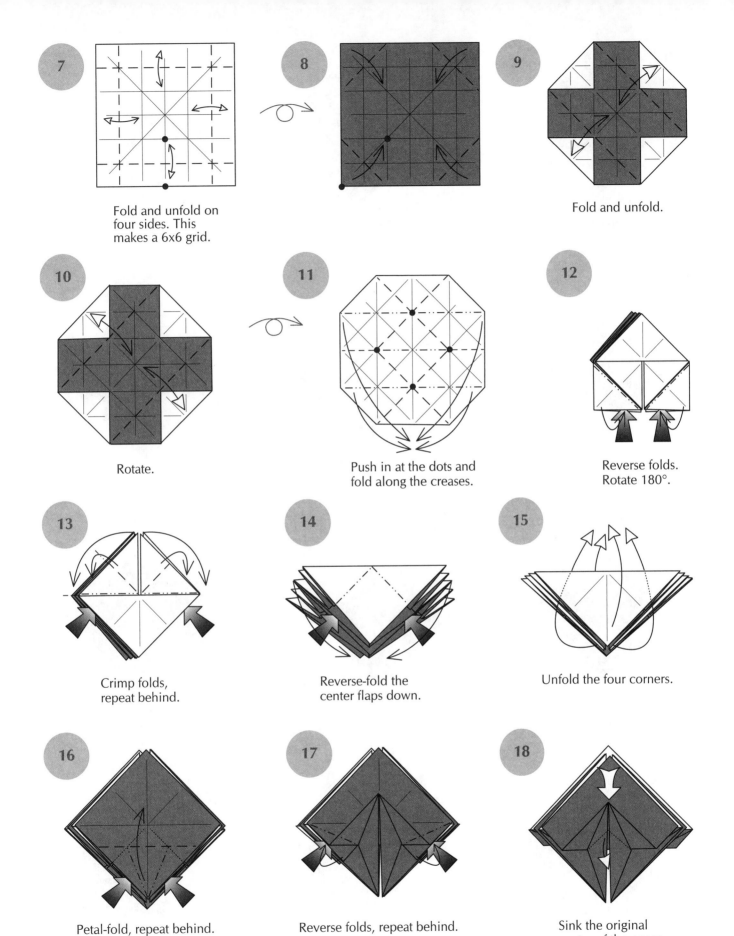

7 Fold and unfold on four sides. This makes a 6x6 grid.

8

9 Fold and unfold.

10 Rotate.

11 Push in at the dots and fold along the creases.

12 Reverse folds. Rotate 180°.

13 Crimp folds, repeat behind.

14 Reverse-fold the center flaps down.

15 Unfold the four corners.

16 Petal-fold, repeat behind.

17 Reverse folds, repeat behind.

18 Sink the original center of the paper.

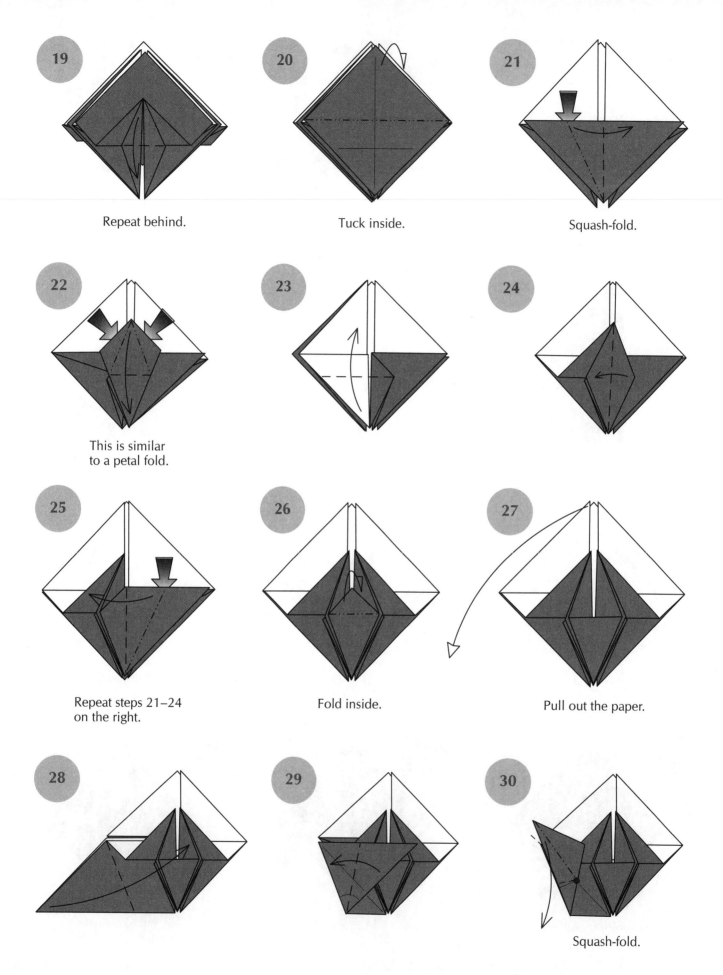

19 Repeat behind.

20 Tuck inside.

21 Squash-fold.

22 This is similar to a petal fold.

23

24

25 Repeat steps 21–24 on the right.

26 Fold inside.

27 Pull out the paper.

28

29

30 Squash-fold.

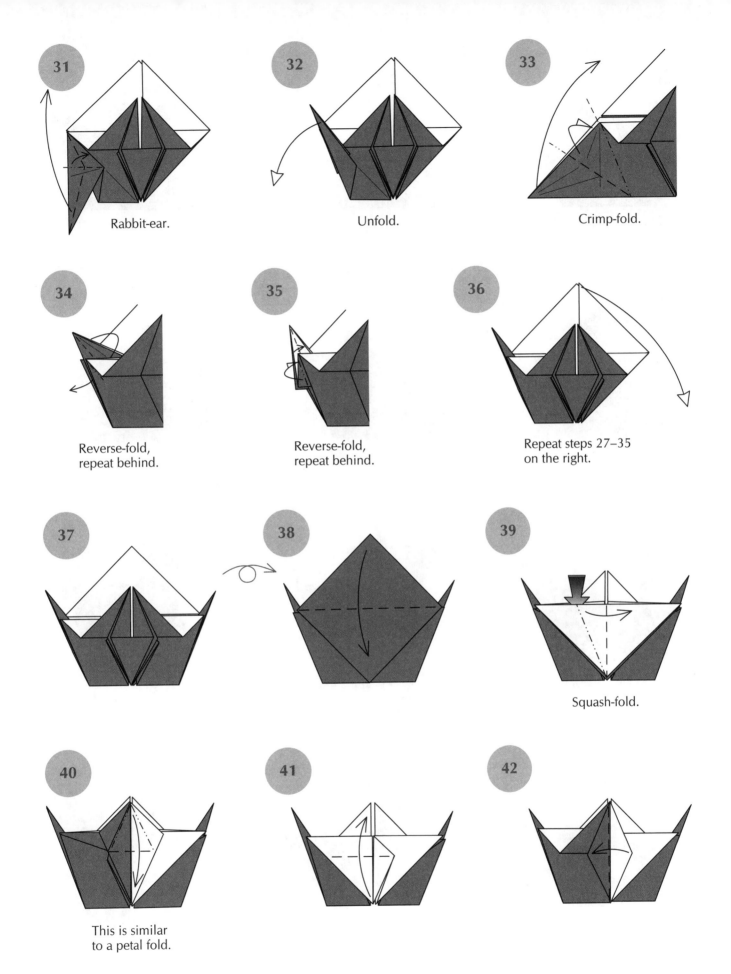

31 Rabbit-ear.

32 Unfold.

33 Crimp-fold.

34 Reverse-fold, repeat behind.

35 Reverse-fold, repeat behind.

36 Repeat steps 27–35 on the right.

37

38

39 Squash-fold.

40 This is similar to a petal fold.

41

42

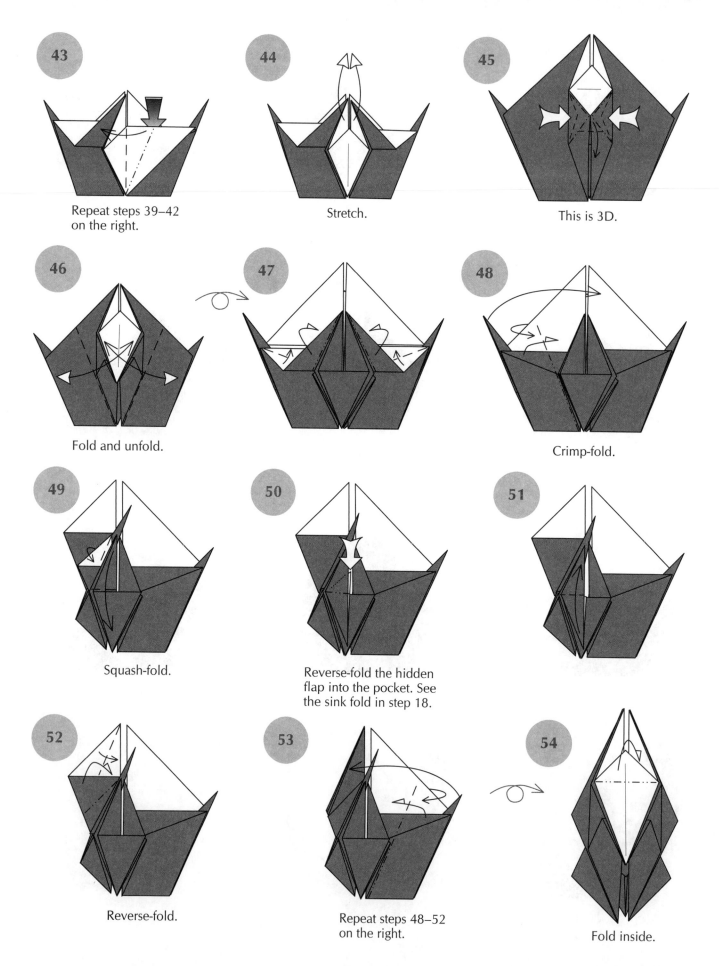

43 Repeat steps 39–42 on the right.

44 Stretch.

45 This is 3D.

46 Fold and unfold.

47

48 Crimp-fold.

49 Squash-fold.

50 Reverse-fold the hidden flap into the pocket. See the sink fold in step 18.

51

52 Reverse-fold.

53 Repeat steps 48–52 on the right.

54 Fold inside.

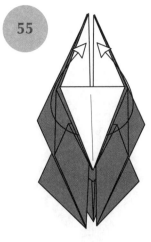

55

This is similar to the double-unwrap-fold.

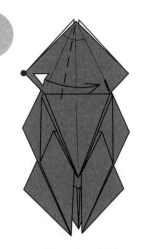

56

Fold and unfold.

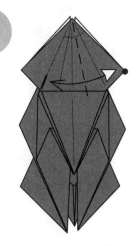

57

Fold and unfold.

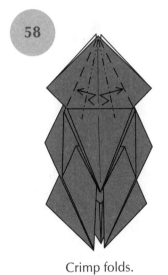

58

Crimp folds.

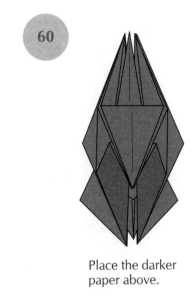

59

Reverse folds.

60

Place the darker paper above.

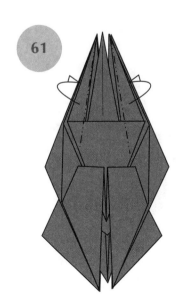

61

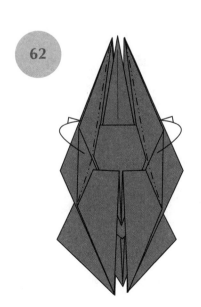

62

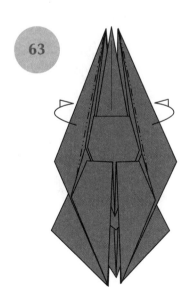

63

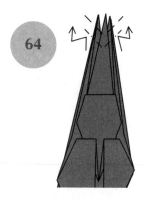

64

Reverse folds.

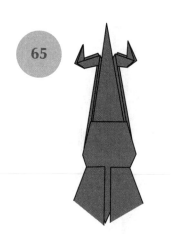

65

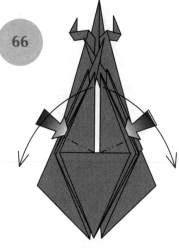

66

Reverse folds.

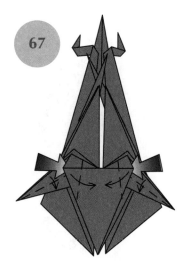

67

Squash folds.

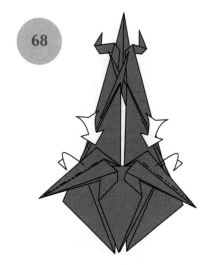

68

Reverse folds.

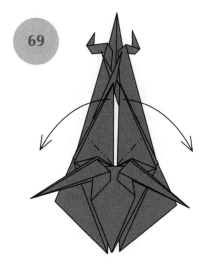

69

Make reverse folds with
small spread-squash-folds.

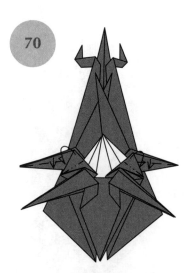

70

Reverse folds,
repeat behind.

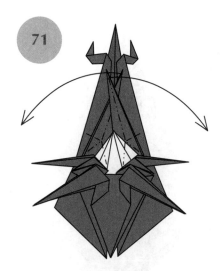

71

Double-rabbit-ear
the two front legs.

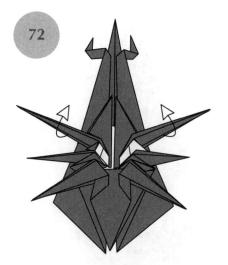

72

Pull out the top layers,
repeat behind.

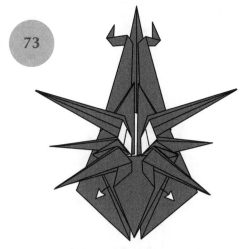

73 Pull out some paper.

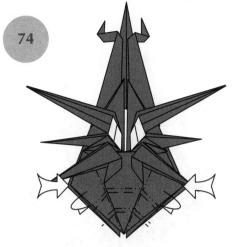

74 Shape the tail.

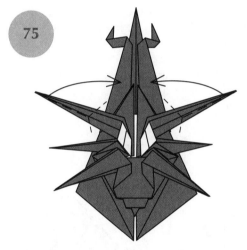

75 Rabbit-ear the front legs.

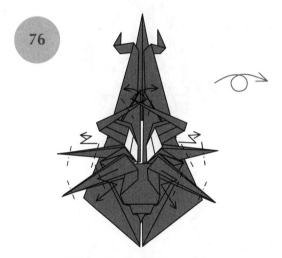

76 Shape the legs with simple mountain and valley folds.

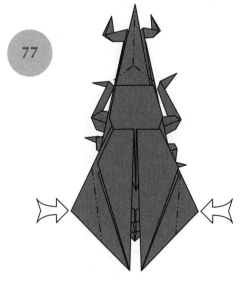

77 By folding the rabbit ear, the weevil's head will point towards the ground. Sink the wings.

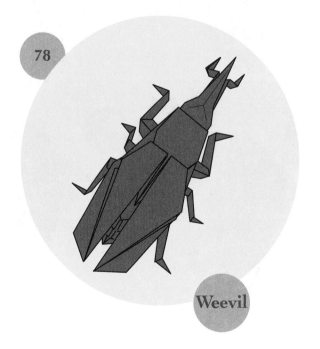

78 Weevil

Asparagus Beetle

The Asparagus Beetle is a rather small bug that is about one-fourth of an inch in size. They usually have dark wing covers with reddish borders, yellowish patches and a reddish thorax with a bluish black head. These bugs like to feed on asparagus plants which gives them their famous name.

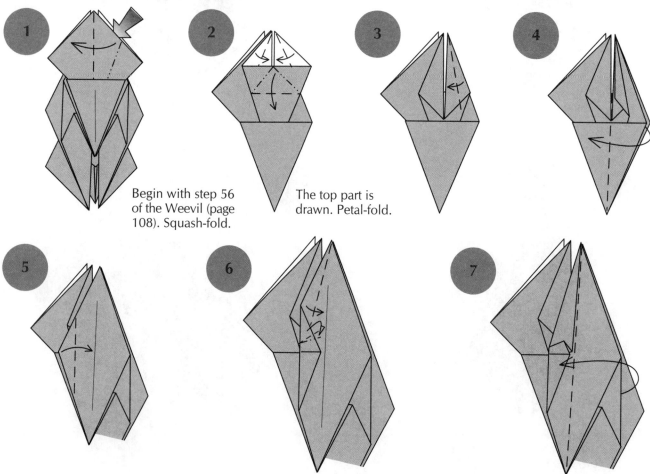

Begin with step 56 of the Weevil (page 108). Squash-fold.

The top part is drawn. Petal-fold.

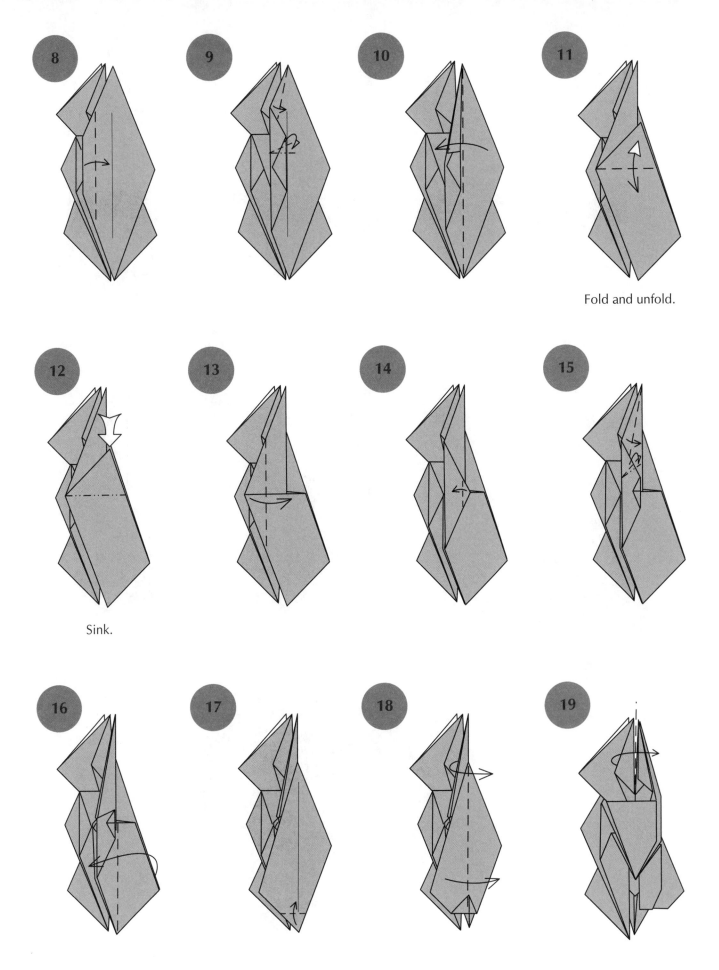

8

9

10

11

Fold and unfold.

12

Sink.

13

14

15

16

17

18

19

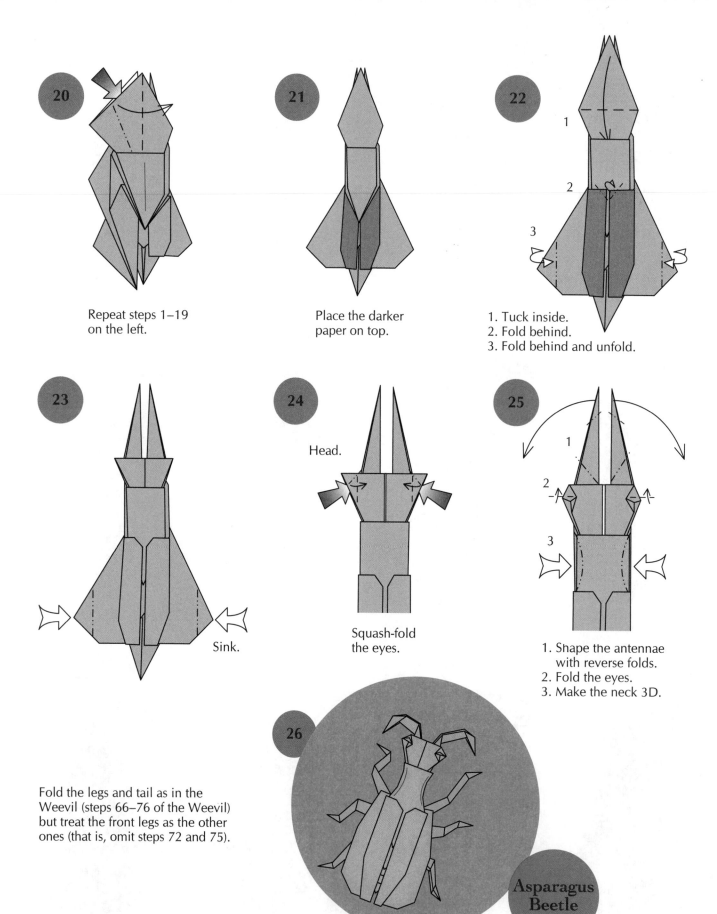

20

Repeat steps 1–19
on the left.

21

Place the darker
paper on top.

22

1. Tuck inside.
2. Fold behind.
3. Fold behind and unfold.

23

Sink.

24

Head.

Squash-fold
the eyes.

25

1. Shape the antennae
   with reverse folds.
2. Fold the eyes.
3. Make the neck 3D.

26

Fold the legs and tail as in the
Weevil (steps 66–76 of the Weevil)
but treat the front legs as the other
ones (that is, omit steps 72 and 75).

Asparagus
Beetle

Centipede

The Centipede (literally "One Hundred Foot"), has a long snakelike body with one pair of legs per body segment. Depending on their species, they can have from less than 20 up to 300 legs. While most species are relatively small, the Peruvian Giant Centipede can reach up to 12 inches in length.

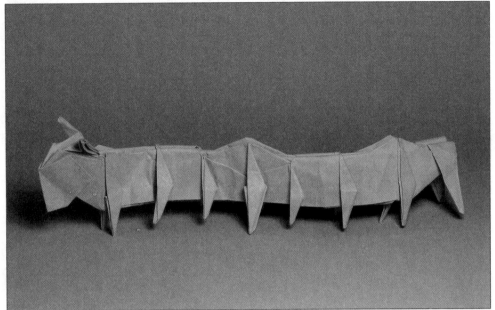

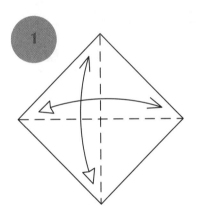

1

Fold and unfold.

2

Fold to the center.

3

Unfold.

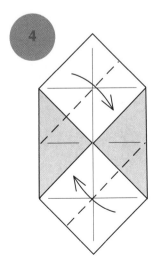

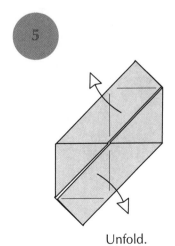

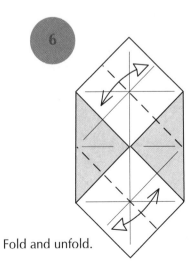

4

5

Unfold.

6

Fold and unfold.

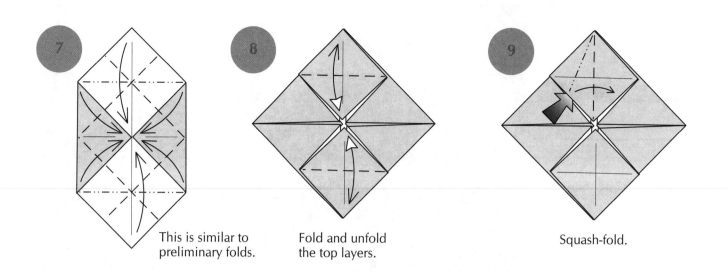

7 This is similar to preliminary folds.

8 Fold and unfold the top layers.

9 Squash-fold.

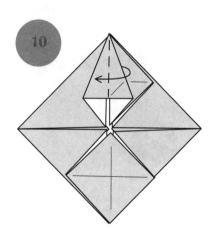

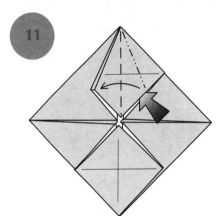

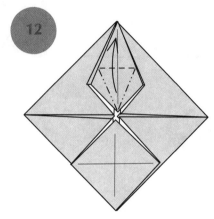

10

11 Repeat steps 9–10 on the right.

12 Petal-fold.

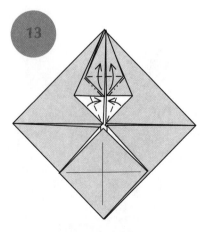

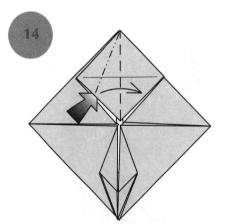

13 Squash folds. Rotate 180°.

14 Repeat steps 9–13.

15 Fold to the center and unfold.

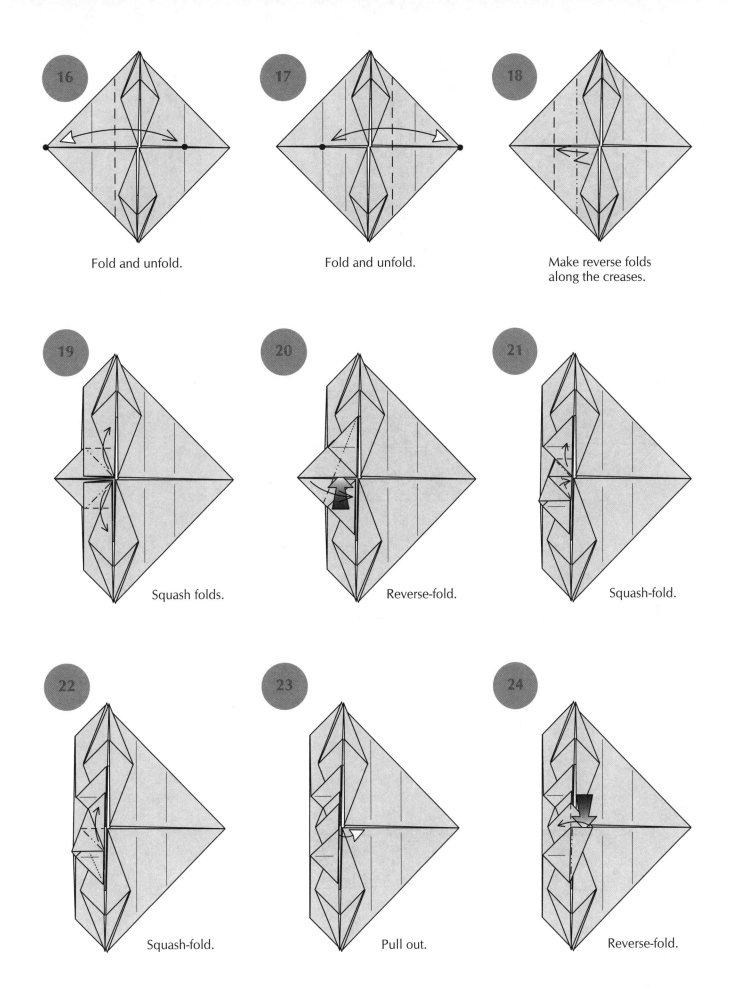

16 Fold and unfold.

17 Fold and unfold.

18 Make reverse folds along the creases.

19 Squash folds.

20 Reverse-fold.

21 Squash-fold.

22 Squash-fold.

23 Pull out.

24 Reverse-fold.

Centipede 121

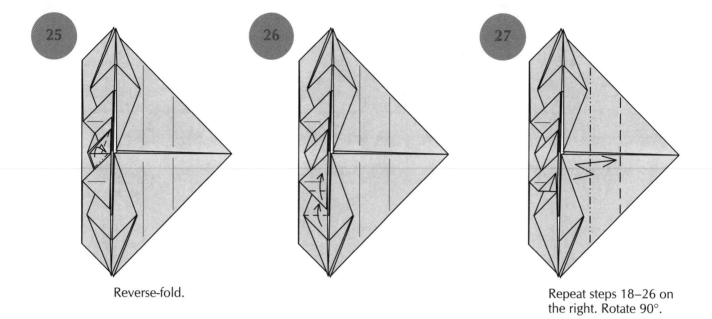

25 Reverse-fold.

27 Repeat steps 18–26 on the right. Rotate 90°.

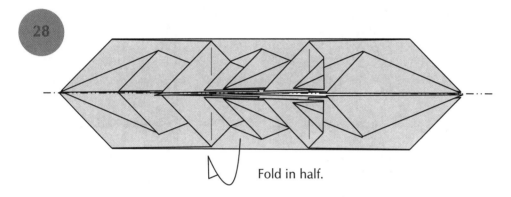

28 Fold in half.

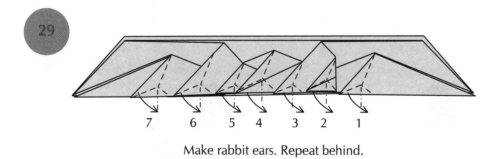

29

7   6   5   4   3   2   1

Make rabbit ears. Repeat behind.

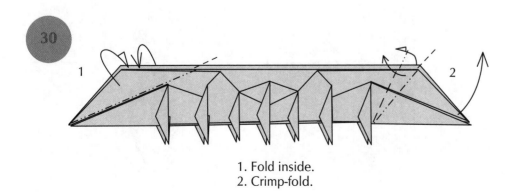

30

1
2

1. Fold inside.
2. Crimp-fold.

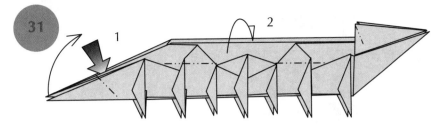

31

1. Reverse-fold the inner layer.
2. Fold inside and squash-fold by the head. Repeat behind.

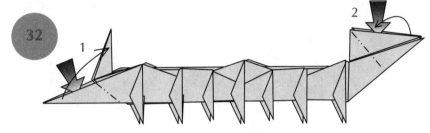

32

1. Reverse-fold.
2. Reverse-fold.

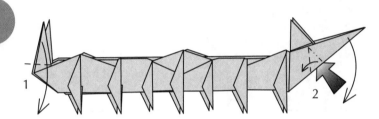

33

1. Repeat behind.
2. Outside-reverse-fold and spread.

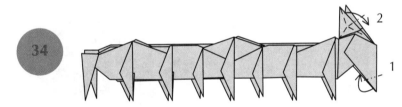

34

1. Reverse-fold.
2. Rabbit-ear, repeat behind.

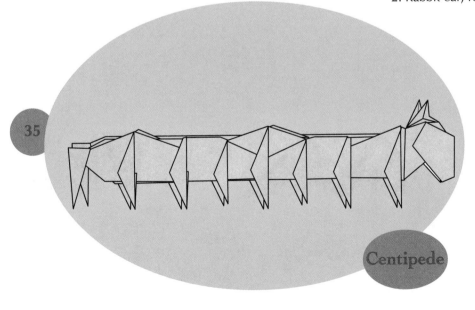

35

Centipede

Spider

Spiders (arachnids) can be found all over the world. There are thousands of different kinds of spiders ranging in size and color. A female spider lays more than a thousand eggs at a time. When the eggs hatch, the baby spiders look like tiny versions of their full grown parents.

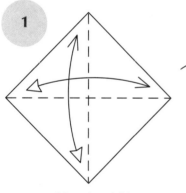

Fold and unfold.

Fold and unfold on the edge.

Fold and unfold on the diagonal.

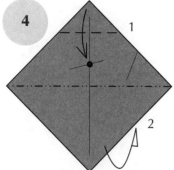

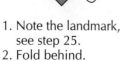
1. Note the landmark, see step 25.
2. Fold behind.

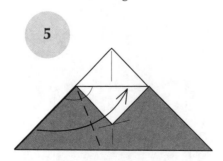

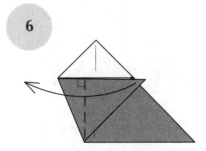

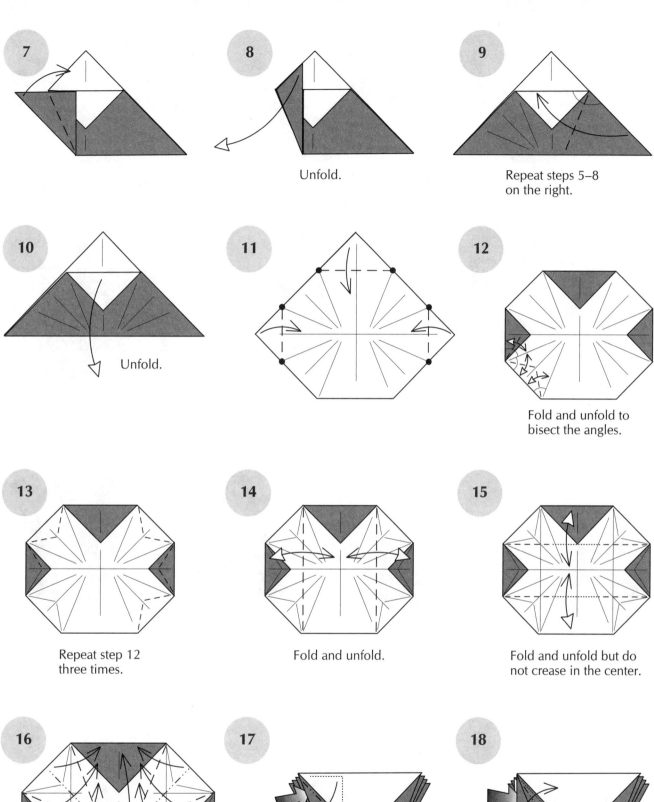

7

8

Unfold.

9

Repeat steps 5–8
on the right.

10

Unfold.

11

12

Fold and unfold to
bisect the angles.

13

Repeat step 12
three times.

14

Fold and unfold.

15

Fold and unfold but do
not crease in the center.

16

Collapse along the creases.

17

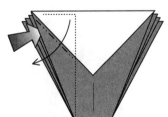

Reverse-fold along
the creases.

18

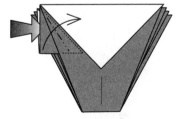

Reverse-fold along
the creases.

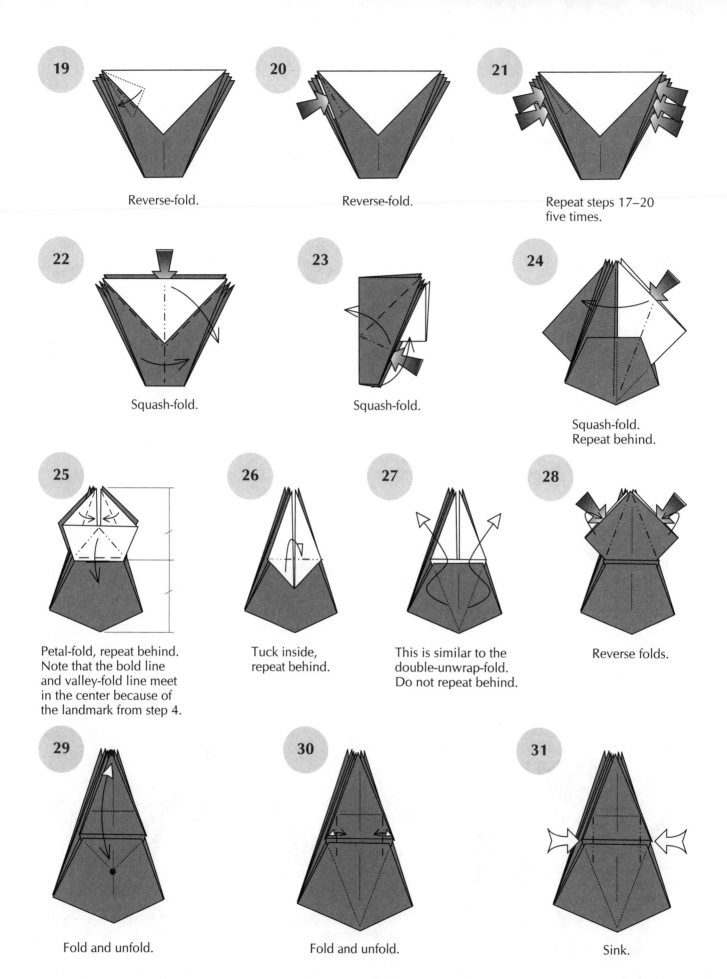

19 Reverse-fold.

20 Reverse-fold.

21 Repeat steps 17–20 five times.

22 Squash-fold.

23 Squash-fold.

24 Squash-fold. Repeat behind.

25 Petal-fold, repeat behind. Note that the bold line and valley-fold line meet in the center because of the landmark from step 4.

26 Tuck inside, repeat behind.

27 This is similar to the double-unwrap-fold. Do not repeat behind.

28 Reverse folds.

29 Fold and unfold.

30 Fold and unfold.

31 Sink.

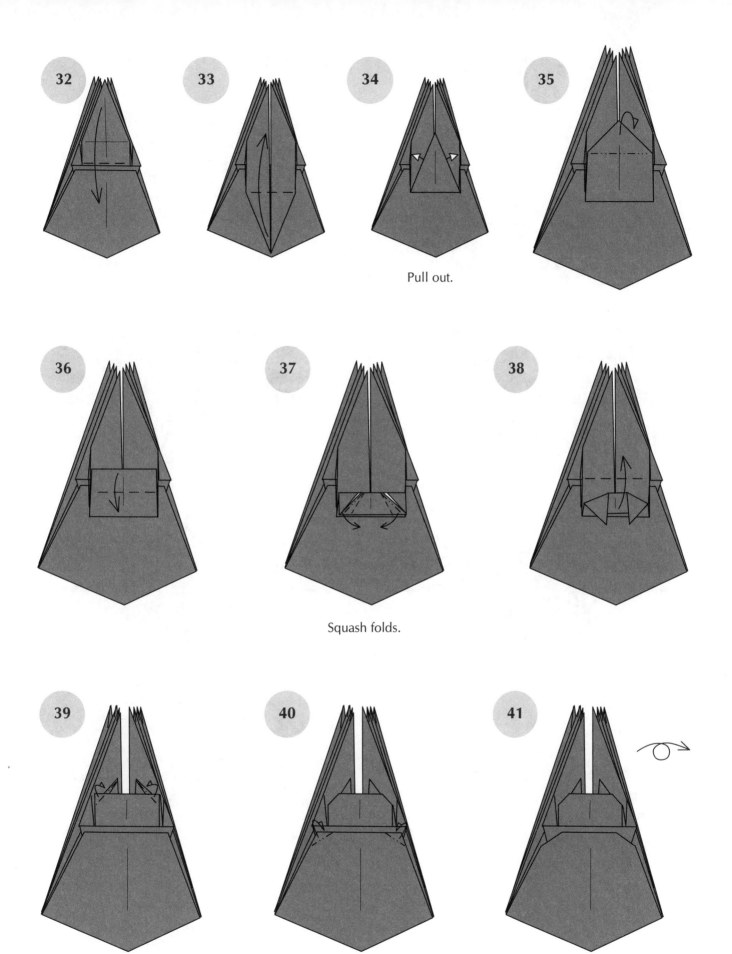

32

33

34

Pull out.

35

36

37

Squash folds.

38

39

40

41

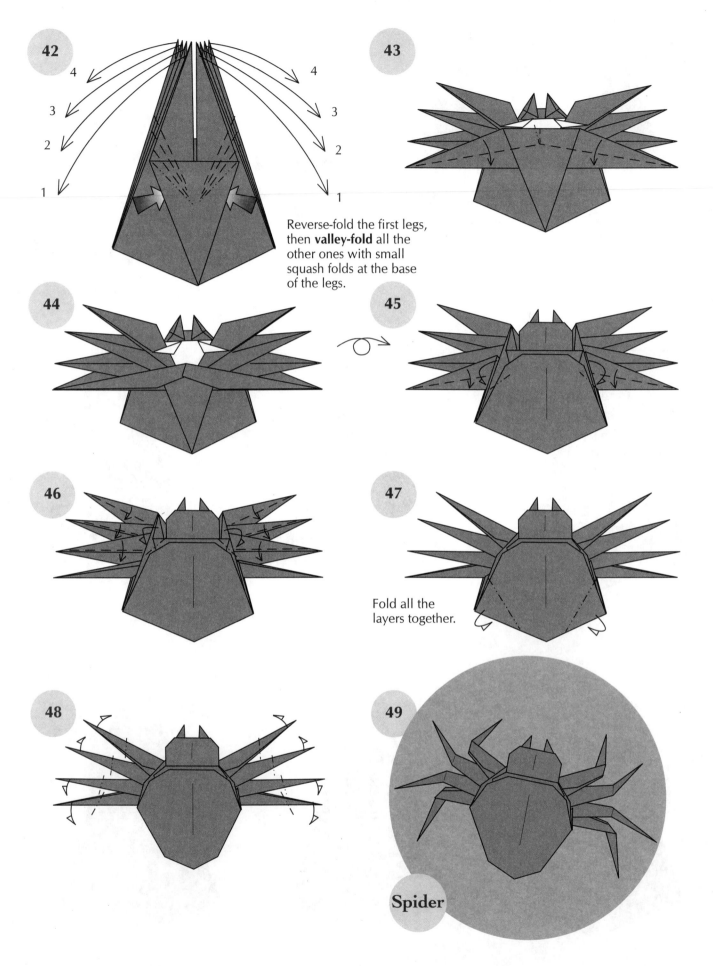

42

4 4
3 3
2 2
1 1

Reverse-fold the first legs, then **valley-fold** all the other ones with small squash folds at the base of the legs.

43

44

45

46

47

Fold all the layers together.

48

49

Spider